THE **ALL** FACTOR

JIM CREWS

THE ALL FACTOR

UNLOCKING THE PROMISES OF GOD FOR YOUR LIFE

To my beautiful wife, Tara —
For over thirty years, you've been my true partner in life, through every joy and every challenge. Thank you for being my prayer warrior, my battle buddy, my confidant, and my favorite copilot on this great adventure. I am so grateful to God for bringing you into my life.

CONTENTS

INTRODUCTION

THE GREATEST
OF ALL TIME

IT'S SUNDAY IN October. It is the greatest month of the year for sports fans. Almost every professional sport is in season. The NFL, the NBA, the NHL, the MLB, the MLS, just to name a few. My son, Josiah, and I, along with my honorary son, Korbin, step into Buffalo Wild Wings for a quick lunch after a great morning of church gatherings.

It's my first time to experience this place. The aroma of the food about knocks me off my feet, but then I notice something even greater than the tasty smell of barbecue, multiple televisions on every wall, each one showing a different game. It is a sports fan's dream.

The restaurant is full of customers wearing different sports jerseys, representing their favorite team, cheering and yelling their lungs out. A couple of guys next to us are in a heated discussion. One of them says with a raised voice, "Hands down, LeBron is the GOAT." His friend says back to him with even more passion in his voice, "It's not even close. Michael is the GOAT and will forever be the GOAT."

If you are not familiar with this expression, you might consider it an insult, but it's actually a huge compliment. The expression stands for the *greatest of all time*. These two guys were engaged in one of the most hotly debated topics of our time. Who is the *greatest of all time* player in NBA history? Many people argue that the GOAT is LeBron James. Others say the GOAT is Michael Jordan, but as the author of this book, I feel compelled to share my opinion on this hot topic. There's no contest about who the GOAT of the NBA is. It's Steph Curry. He's the Lord's warrior.

This concept of the *greatest of all time* is not just limited to speaking about sports or athletes. People discuss and debate all kinds of GOATs. Who is the *GOAT* of American presidents? Who is the *GOAT* rock band? How about the *GOAT* movie? (By the way, if you are ever hosting a party at your house, these kinds of questions are guaranteed to always get your guests talking to each other.)

What we find in the Bible is that discussions over the *greatest of all time* aren't just a modern idea. The first-century Jewish community also had its own debate for the *greatest of all time*, except it wasn't over a sports figure. It was regarding the commandments of God.

In Jewish culture, commandments are very important rules that God gave to help people live good, meaningful, godly lives. These commandments cover many aspects of daily life, such as how to treat others, how to celebrate special holidays, and how to stay connected to God. For Jewish people, following these commandments is a way to show love for God and to remember their history and traditions. They are a central part of their faith and daily life.

As you read the Bible, especially the part that is referred to as the Old Testament, you will observe God had many commandments he called the Jewish people to follow. Most biblical scholars believe there are a total of 613 of them (yes, there are more than ten), and a devout Jewish person would know all of those commandments.

This brings us to Jesus and the moment he is pulled into the great debate over what commandment is the *greatest of all time* commandment. And I believe his answer is one of the most powerful things that Jesus goes on record to tell us.

> One of the teachers of the law came and heard them debating. Noticing that Jesus had given them a good answer, he asked him, "Of all the commandments, which is the most important?" (MARK 12:28 NIV)

So this teacher of the law is asking Jesus, "What is the *GOAT* commandment?"

This is the surprising part. Jesus, who would typically answer a question by asking a question of his own, actually answers the question and gives his opinion on what is the *greatest of all time* commandment.

> "The most important one," answered Jesus, "is this: 'Hear, O Israel: The Lord our God, the Lord is one. Love the Lord your God with all your heart and with all your soul and with all your mind and with all your strength.'" (MARK 12:29–30 NIV)

Read this again, but a little slower this time.
Notice how the word *all* is repeated.
It's an important word. We will come back to this in a moment.
He goes on to say,

> The second is this, love your neighbor as yourself. There is no commandment greater than these. (MARK 12:31 NIV)

> "Well said, teacher." The man replied, "You are right in saying that God is one and there is no other but him. To love him with all of your heart, with all your understanding, with all of your strength, and to love your neighbor as yourself is more important than all burnt offerings and sacrifices." When Jesus saw that he had answered wisely, he said to him, "You are not far from the kingdom of God." And from then on, no one dared ask him any more questions. (MARK 12:32–34 NIV)

The crowd was stunned by Jesus's clear response.

The debate was over.

In addition to directly answering the question of what the GOAT commandment is, Jesus even gives this teacher something of a compliment, which did not happen very often for these teachers who questioned Jesus. Jesus tells him that he is *not far from the kingdom of God*.

In other words, "you are on the edge of experiencing the most powerful way to live, with God ruling as king of your life." That's what the *kingdom of God* is. When God reigns as king of your life, that's when you truly flourish in life.

Why did the teacher of the law stop short of experiencing the kingdom of God? He still needed to put his faith in Jesus, and he wasn't quite ready to do that.

It's important to point out that when Jesus was talking to the crowd about this commandment, they knew exactly what he was saying. They would have all learned this commandment as children. The first prayer a Jewish child memorizes is this commandment. It's also the last thing a devout Jewish person hears before dying. They're saying this each morning and repeating this each night. It's part of the Jewish Torah that's commonly referred to as *the Shema*.[1] It's found in the sixth chapter of the book of Deuteronomy in the Hebrew Scriptures.

When Jesus starts saying this commandment, everyone listening would be following him word for word. It is more than a prayer. It is a pledge. It would be equivalent to an American hearing someone reciting the Pledge of Allegiance. In my generation, this was the first thing we learned in school. Every morning, we would stand, place our hand over our hearts, look at the flag in our classroom, and hear the leader say, "Salute. Pledge." (Some of you, just reading those two words right now, have already started saying the pledge in your minds.)

Even though you're not in fourth grade anymore, if you heard someone around you start saying, "I pledge allegiance to the flag of the United States of America," you would more than likely move your lips to the words or maybe even start saying it out loud along with them.

This is exactly what the people would have been doing when Jesus starts quoting the Shema to them.

Now, Jesus says a lot of things in the Gospels, but I think if he's going on record to say this is the *GOAT* commandment, we ought to lean in and look at this really, really closely.

> "The *most important* one," answered Jesus, "is this: 'Hear, O Israel: The Lord our God, the Lord is one. Love the Lord your God with *all* your heart and with *all* your soul and with *all* your mind and with *all* your strength.'" (Words have been italicized in this Scripture for emphasis only.)

Before we dive into the details of this *GOAT* commandment and go deep with this word *all*, it's super important we are all on the same page with this word *love*. It's a word tossed around so often in our culture. Many people have different understandings of what love really means. For example, you may say, "I love pizza," or "I love my family," but certainly, you don't love your family the same way you love pizza.

If you really want a great picture of what Jesus means by saying the word *love* in this *GOAT* commandment, I recommend you set this book down, grab a Bible, and read 1 Corinthians 13. The author of this ancient letter is the apostle Paul. He wrote to this church in Corinth and really wanted them to understand what God has in mind when he uses this word *love*.

Here are some highlights of how love is described in this chapter.

LOVE IS...

- **PATIENT:** Love is slow to anger and enduring.
- **KIND:** Love is gentle and considerate, showing compassion.
- **NOT SELF-SEEKING:** Love is unselfish and prioritizes the needs of others.
- **KEEPS NO RECORD OF WRONGS:** Love does not hold grudges or remember past offenses.
- **NOT EASILY ANGERED:** Love is forgiving and does not hold onto anger easily.
- **PERSEVERES:** Love endures through challenges and remains steadfast.

Chances are, if you've been to a wedding over the last few years, you've probably heard 1 Corinthians 13 quoted. Looking at how *love* is described in this chapter is a great way to better understand the love Jesus is speaking about in this *GOAT* commandment.

This biblical understanding of *love* can be described as a commitment of the will. Most people in our culture who are not familiar with this biblical understanding of *love* will say *love* is more of a *feeling*. Don't misunderstand me. You can absolutely *feel* love, but this biblical understanding of love is so much more than a *feeling*. This love is a pursuit. This love is walking intentionally toward something or someone. This love is committed and loyal.

If you are married, I am sure you understand this to a degree because when you got married, you made vows to your spouse. Vows that involved commitment, pursuit, and intentionality, for better or for worse, for richer or poorer, in sickness and in health.

A big reason why we are seeing so many failed marriages in our culture now is that many couples have lost touch with this understanding of *love* found in the Scriptures. For many people, once that loving *feeling* is gone, they're gone. They leave. They get a divorce. Then they go and try to find that loving *feeling* with someone else. This is a very poor and shallow version of *love*.

Here are some big marriage tips for you:

- Pursue your spouse.
- Be intentional toward your spouse.
- Be committed to your spouse.

So when we read the word *love* in this *GOAT* commandment, it is a word that invokes the commitment, pursuit, and intentionality that goes along with *love*.

When you start thinking about your *love* relationship with God, do you see that commitment? Do you see that pursuit? Do you see that intentionality? That is what Jesus means when he is using the word *love* in this commandment:

> *Love* the Lord your God with *all* your *heart* and with *all* your *soul* and with *all* your *mind* and with *all* your *strength*.

Now it's time to talk about what is the greatest word in this *greatest of all time* commandment:

ALL.

ALL: ὅλος–olos (pronounced "hol'-os")
MEANING: all, whole, completely, fully

We get our English word *holistic* from this word in the Greek language. For example, have you heard of holistic medicine? It's an approach to your healthcare that is beyond just the physical. If you see a holistic doctor, they will approach your medical situation holistically, meaning completely and fully. They are going to check your physical self, your emotional self, your mental self, and sometimes even your spiritual self.

The reason I love using the text from the Gospel of Mark on this *greatest of all time* commandment is because it encompasses all four parts of our being:

- Love God with *all* of your *heart* (emotionally).
- Love God with *all* of your *soul* (spiritually).
- Love God with *all* of your *mind* (mentally).
- Love God with *all* of your *strength* (physically).

Think about it. In these four areas that the *greatest of all time* commandment covers, you have your emotional, mental, spiritual, and physical self represented. These four areas cover all of your being. God created you with four parts of your being. Each part impacts the others. All four of these together make up the whole of who you are.

As we break this down, we need to think about the *all* that Jesus and the *greatest of all time* commandment is inviting us into.

It's not a part-time relationship with God.

It's not some part-time love affair with God.

The call is to love him with our all.

This *greatest of all time* commandment isn't the only place in Scripture where we find a great emphasis put on the word *all*. The Bible actually features the importance of this word in several places. Let me give you a couple of examples:

> How blessed are those who observe His testimonies,
> Who seek Him with all their heart.
> (PSALM 119:2 NASB 1995)

So the blessing is discovered in the all.

> You will seek Me and find Me when you search for Me
> with all your heart. (JEREMIAH 29:13 NASB 1995)

So God will show up, and you will experience him when you
do it with your all.

> The eyes of the Lord search the whole earth in order
> to strengthen those whose hearts are fully committed
> to him. (2 CHRONICLES 16:9 NLT)

So God is on a quest, and he's searching the entire earth for
people that are living in the *all* of God, and when he finds them,
he uses them in powerful ways.

When God uses you in a powerful way like this, it launches
you to a whole new level, a level where you begin experiencing the
wonder and *awe* of God. You start seeing how awesome God is.

Here is how I like to say it.

When you're living in the *all* of God, you start experiencing the
awe of God.

Let me ask this question.

If someone you know was asked to describe your relationship with
God, would they use the word *powerful?* When they think about
you and your faith in God, when they think about your pursuit of
Jesus, would they choose the word *powerful?*

If we live out this life the way Jesus called us to live it out, I am
convinced our lives will be described by others as *powerful.*

If you look at the things that Jesus did in his life and the things
that Jesus said would happen in our lives, if you study the experiences of the early church in the book of Acts, and if you read all the
letters Paul wrote to the churches of his time, you have to conclude

a life completely and fully given to God is going to lead to *powerful* experiences with God.

For the first five years after I made the decision to follow Jesus, I wasn't living in the *all* of God, and nothing *powerful* was happening in me or through me. I went to church on most Sundays. I would read my Bible a few days a week, but there was something noticeably missing. I just didn't see the miracles happening. I would come to church, and I would listen to my pastor speak and share his personal miracle stories. I would hear how God was doing these amazing things in his life.

I remember spending many days wondering, *Why aren't these things happening in my life?* The more I poured myself into the Scriptures, the more I began to realize I wasn't giving God my *all*; I was just giving him some. And if you're reading this and you've been following Jesus for a while, you know there's a big difference between *some* and *all*.

Get Your Motor Running

NOW, I'M NOT a mechanic, but I have a lot of mechanic friends. And one of the things I have learned about engines is different engines have different kinds of horsepower and different numbers of cylinders. I want you to think of this *GOAT* commandment as a type of motor for your spiritual life. According to the Gospel of Mark, it is like a four-cylinder motor, with four distinct compartments: heart, soul, mind, and strength.

If you know anything about cars, when your car is not running on all cylinders, it becomes problematic. If one cylinder goes down in a four-cylinder motor, you're basically losing one-fourth of your engine power. And most mechanics will tell you if you don't address the issue with the one cylinder, the whole motor is in jeopardy of actually being corrupted.

Have you ever heard the expression "He's not firing on all cylinders"? You might even say that about yourself before you drink some coffee in the morning. We use this expression because we are trying to communicate that we are not operating at full power.

Think about that as you think about what Jesus is saying is the *greatest of all time* commandment. Your life is like a four-cylinder motor. In order for you to start experiencing God in a powerful way, you have to pay attention to all four areas Jesus mentions in this commandment.

- Your heart
- Your soul
- Your mind
- Your strength

Without putting your all in all four areas, you will not experience the fullness of life Jesus intended you to live.

Unfortunately for me, for the first five years of having a relationship with Jesus, I was not firing on all cylinders for Jesus, and it showed.

The promises of God were eluding me.

The awesomeness of God was absent from me.

It wasn't until I made a decision to love God with my *all*, in *all* four of these areas, that I started really walking in the promises of God and experiencing powerful moments in my faith. It took giving my *all* in *all* to finally experience the breakthrough I had been praying for in my life.

How about you?

How's your spiritual motor running these days?

Are you firing on *all* cylinders?

Caleb: The Wizard of *All*

LET ME INTRODUCE you to a man from the Hebrew Scriptures who embodied this all factor so well.

His name is Caleb.

When I get to heaven, there are so many people I'm going to want to have a conversation with. One of the first on my list is Caleb. There is something so special about the life Caleb lived when he was on earth.

One of the biggest highlights of his life was when he was chosen to be one of the twelve explorers of the Promised Land. The Israelites were in their pursuit of the Promised Land. There were twelve explorers, or *spies* as some call them, who were sent into this new land. As they explored the land, they discovered there were giants in this new land. Ten of the explorers came back and said, "We can't take this land. There are giants there." But the other two explorers, Joshua and Caleb, had a different perspective.

Caleb responded with such giant faith. To paraphrase his response, he said, "Sure, there are these guys that are twice as big as we are. But you know, I don't care. They could be ten times bigger than we are. We have God on our side. So if God is on our side, we will always have the victory. Because if God is for us, who can be against us?"

That's Caleb!

Caleb was a guy that you just wanted to hang out with because he had such strong confidence in God.

And listen to what God says about him.

> But as for My servant Caleb, because he has had a different spirit and has followed Me fully, I will bring him into the land which he entered, and his descendants shall take possession of it. (NUMBERS 14:24 NASB)

Caleb had a different spirit. (I love that description.)

What made his spirit different? It was because he followed God *fully*.

To follow him fully means to follow him utterly, absolutely, without any reservation.

So the promises of God were given to Caleb because he had fully given himself over to God. He entered into the promises of God because of his *all* factor.

Fast-forward a few chapters, we learn what is probably the most important part of Caleb's story.

> None of the men who came up from Egypt, from twenty years old and upward, shall see the land which I swore to Abraham, to Isaac, and to Jacob; for they did not follow Me fully, except Caleb the son of Jephunneh the Kenizzite and Joshua the son of Nun; for they have followed the Lord fully. (NUMBERS 32:11–12 NASB 1995)

Did you catch that?

None of the other men made it in.

Only Caleb and Joshua entered into the Promised Land. Why? Because they were living their lives in the *all* of God.

Here is the big takeaway we can all learn from Caleb.

The key to unlocking the door to the promises of God for your life is found in the word *all*.

The Price We Pay
for Living Halfway

THE FINAL BOOK of the Bible, known as the book of Revelation, features what reads like a series of heavenly Yelp reviews of seven different churches written by Jesus himself. (These reviews are found in chapters 2 and 3.) One of the most critical reviews is given to the church in Laodicea. This review contains a warning that I believe is relevant not just for Laodicea but for all of us.

> To the angel of the church in Laodicea, write: These are the words of the Amen, the faithful and true witness, the ruler of God's creation. I know your deeds, that you are neither cold nor hot. I wish you were either one or the other! So, because you are lukewarm—neither hot nor cold—I am about to spit you out of my mouth. You say, 'I am rich; I have acquired wealth and do not need a thing.' But you do not realize that you are wretched, pitiful, poor, blind and naked. I counsel you to buy

from me gold refined in the fire, so you can become
rich; and white clothes to wear, so you can cover your
shameful nakedness; and salve to put on your eyes, so
you can see. (REVELATION 3:14–18 NIV)

Jesus uses the term *lukewarm* to describe this church. They were
neither hot nor cold. He is making it abundantly clear that being
in the middle is a terrible place to be.

Imagine if Jesus used an analogy of a cup instead of temperature
to describe the condition of this lukewarm church. Jesus would
say something like, "Your cup is only half full. I'd rather there be
nothing in your cup at all rather than you just being half full (or
half empty, depending on how you see it)."

Whether you see the cup as half full or half empty, the indisput-
able fact is there is room for more.

The call of God is to live for him with your glass full to the brim.
Not some. Not part. But full. And if you don't have this *all* factor,
this *hot* factor, this hot pursuit of God (if you want to call it that),
where you're *all* in, then Jesus is giving a warning that it would be
better for you not to be in at all.

Let me tell you about my own breakthrough experience with this.

I was five years saved and had just finished my freshman year of
college, living back with my parents for the summer. I had to decide
where I was going to live for my sophomore year of college. I had
two different groups of guys asking me if I would consider getting
an apartment with them. One group of guys was part of my dorm
during my freshman year. These were great guys I had a ton of fun
with. Unfortunately, the fun I experienced with them was not godly
at all. My freshman year of college involved a lot of parties and a
lot of weed. These guys knew where all the best weed was in town,
and they knew where all the good parties were on the weekends.
The other group of guys asking me to live with them were these

amazing Christian guys who I went to high school with and who I had been occasionally attending an on-campus Bible study with. They knew I had a relationship with God, but they didn't know how much I was partying.

I remember this hot summer day swimming in the pool at my parent's house. I was trying to make this decision: Who do I live with? And I knew myself. If I chose the Christian guys, I was going to do a lot better in pursuing God. But if I chose the party guys, I might stumble some more, but man, I was going to have a lot of fun. I was just going back and forth, creating a pros and cons list in my head. Remember the cartoons where the angel is on one shoulder, and the devil is on the other shoulder, and they are both talking to you? That is exactly what was happening to me at that moment.

Then, out of nowhere, comes this loud voice. I can't say that I heard this voice audibly, but I did hear it clearly, and I knew it was the voice of God. He said, "Jim, you're either for me, or you're against me. Be *all* in or don't be in at all." Those words gutted me. For a moment, I thought about what it would look like just to dismiss the thought of the existence of God. What would it look like to live as though God didn't even exist? Do whatever I wanted and "party on, dude." Just go for it.

That thought lasted for half a second. I realized in that holy moment that there was no way I could do that. I had experienced enough of God to make it impossible to pretend he didn't exist. He had already done so many incredible things in my life. The tears started pouring out of me in the pool that day. This loving ultimatum changed my life. I knew I only had one choice to make, and that was to be *all in*. I jumped out of the pool, dried off, and made the phone call that would get my motor running correctly. I called my Christian friends and said, "Count me in as one of your roommates."

That was the first step. Then I prayed and asked God to show me what else I needed to do to take this cup that was half full and fill it up to the top. And he showed me.

I got plugged into a local church. I didn't just show up for service on Sunday. I got involved. I started serving. I started waking up early to read the Bible and asked God daily to move in my life. I started doing everything I could to give God my *all*. I didn't want to be God *vomit*. It's weird to say it that way, but that's how Jesus describes living halfway for God. And let me tell you, when I made that decision to live in the *all*, breakthrough happened. The miracles that I'd been wanting started happening. The voice of God became super real to me. Why? What changed? The change was that I decided to live in the *all* of my *love* for God. It changed everything.

Let me give you one more feature of this warning, and it involves a real-life example from one of the ancient kings of Judah. His name was Amaziah.

So here is a little history lesson on Israel. They had a little division going on. They have a northern kingdom and a southern kingdom. The northern kingdom was known as Israel. The southern kingdom was known as Judah. And the kings of Judah tended to be godlier than the kings of Israel.

And then in 2 Chronicles 25, we read about what appears to be a godly king, King Amaziah.

> Amaziah was twenty-five years old when he became king, and he reigned in Jerusalem twenty-nine years. His mother's name was Jehoaddan; she was from Jerusalem. He did what was right in the eyes of the Lord, but not wholeheartedly. (2 CHRONICLES 25:1–2 NIV)

> Amaziah called the people of Judah together and assigned them, according to their families, to commanders

of thousands and commanders of hundreds for all of Judah and Benjamin. He then mustered those twenty years old or more and found that there were three hundred thousand men fit for military service, able to handle the spear and shield. He also hired a hundred thousand fighting men from Israel for a hundred talents of silver. But a man of God came to him and said, "Your Majesty, these troops from Israel must not march with you, for the Lord is not with Israel—not with any of the people of Ephraim. Even if you go and fight courageously in battle, God will overthrow you before the enemy, for God has the power to help or to overthrow." Amaziah asked the man of God, "But what about the hundred talents I paid for these Israelite troops?" The man of God replied, "The Lord can give you much more than that." (2 CHRONICLES 25:5–11 NIV)

I believe God has a word for someone reading this right now.

Maybe there is a deal that you invested in. Maybe you even feel God spoke a word to you, saying, "This is a bad deal," but you invested anyway. Now there is this internal struggle going on inside you, "But I invested. I put down the deposit."

I really feel God speaking a revelation through this passage, "Cut your losses and know that I will take care of you. Don't continue going down with the deal that is a bad deal because it's going to go from bad to worse." I'm going to quote to you what this man of God quoted to Amaziah: *"The Lord can give you much more than that."* Trust him and just cut your losses. It was a bad deal. Next time, take some extra time to pray about it before you put down the deposit.

So Amaziah dismissed the troops who had come to him from Ephraim and sent them home. They were

furious with Judah and left for home in a great rage.
Amaziah then marshaled his strength and led his army
to the Valley of Salt, where he killed ten thousand men
of Seir. (2 CHRONICLES 25:10–11 NIV)

King Amaziah got his victory. He listened to the man of God.
But here's the danger zone of being half full or part-time. It left
room for compromise.

When Amaziah returned from slaughtering the
Edomites, he brought back the gods of the people of
Seir. He set them up as his own gods, bowed down to
them, and burned sacrifices to them. The anger of the
Lord burned against Amaziah, and he sent a prophet
to him, who said, "Why do you consult this people's
gods, which could not save their own people from your
hand?" While he was still speaking, the king said to
him, "Have we appointed you an adviser to the king?
Stop! Why be struck down?" So the prophet stopped
but said, "I know that God has determined to destroy
you, because you have done this and have not listened
to my counsel." (2 CHRONICLES 25:14–16 NIV)

And that's exactly what happened. Amaziah was destroyed.
This is a cautionary tale for all of us.
What did the part-time relationship with God cost him? Everything!
Not being completely full of God left enough room for Amaziah
to place other things in his life that were ungodly, ultimately causing him to drift away from God and open the door for destruction
against his life.
This is what I've discovered: Without being full to the brim with

God, it's easy to be swept away by other things in our culture. This is why you see many people who supposedly love God, people who supposedly follow Jesus, but are continually practicing ungodly things. When you're living with your cup half full, it's easy to say yes to ungodly things in the emptiness of the cup. And if you're not careful, it'll sweep you right into the current of our culture, which is heading for more and more ungodliness, and when this happens, you become compromised.

There are a lot of people of God, a lot of so-called followers of Jesus, who are living compromised lifestyles in their faith, and they're miserable, and they're frustrated.

I know because that was me for so many years.

It's a frustrating feeling knowing God has so much potential for your life, but you're not living in that potential. You're not living in his promises and experiencing a powerful life.

Being a cup half full for God doesn't work. You not only miss out on the promises of God but also give the devil a lot of room in the emptiness to scheme and sabotage your life.

You have to understand that a part-time Christian can't defeat a full-time devil.

The enemy of your soul is ruthless and relentless against your life. If you're just part-time, you are going to be swept off your feet every time you have a face-off with him. The only way to take down giants in your life is by living full-time and in the *all* factor, just as Caleb did.

The Splash Zone

L ET ME TELL you something so awesome about this *greatest of all time* commandment.

When you are *loving* God with your *all*, not only do your giants fall but also your neighbors are loved.

There is a reason the *greatest of all time* commandment has a second part to it.

> The second is this, love your neighbor as yourself. There is no commandment greater than these. (MARK 12:31 NIV)

Jesus did something that no other rabbi before him had ever done. He took this commandment about loving your neighbor, another very familiar Jewish commandment found in the book of Leviticus from the Hebrew Scriptures, and he bundled it with loving God. If you think of your love for God as this vertical relationship (you being here on earth and God being in heaven above) and your love for your neighbor being this horizontal relationship (you standing alongside your neighbor), these two loves together form a cross.

The more our lives are saturated with the unconditional sacrificial love of God, poured out for us on the cross, the more we are able to give this unconditional sacrificial love to our neighbors.

This *all* factor increases our capacity to love our neighbors, even the difficult ones.

Not everyone who is your neighbor is easy to love.

Does a name come to your mind when you think of a difficult person in your life?

We all have some very difficult people we have to deal with in our lives. Maybe a few? How about a dozen? You get the point.

Let's just be real and honest. It's hard to love people who are acting unloving toward you.

Your neighbor could be that jerk-face boss of yours, the grumpy cashier at the gas station, or it could be your actual neighbor talking about you on the Nextdoor app. These neighbors make it so hard to love them.

When you *love* God with your *all*, it's much easier to love your neighbor. You don't have to focus on loving your neighbor. When the cup is *full* of *love* for God in all four of these areas, the *love* is so abundant that it splashes out on everything and everyone around your life.

Have you ever tried to move a cup that was full to the brim of your favorite beverage? A spillover is inevitable. The same goes for our *love* toward God. There is a spillover effect. It is the great outcome of the great income. The income of loving God with your *all* is an outcome of more love for other people, even the people who are difficult to love.

When you love God fully, you unlock the ability to love people unconditionally. This unconditional love is what I like to call *no-strings-attached, Jesus-style love.*

It is possible to live in a relationship with God that is so full of love that when your enemies are crucifying you, you respond by saying, "Father, forgive them, for they know not what they do" (Luke 23:34 ESV).

It's achievable, but you have to decide. Am I going to obey the *greatest of all time commandment?* Am I going to *love* God with my *all?*

It's Assessment Time

HERE'S WHAT I know about you. Out of all four of these areas Jesus mentions in the Gospel of Mark, there's going to be one where you will say, "That's easy for me." Maybe you would say, "It's easy to give God my *all* with my brain," or, "It's easy to give God my *all* with my emotions." No doubt you will find one area easier than the other three. But let's identify some things before we get any further in this book.

I can't remember where I first saw this exercise, but I have used it for decades now to help people in their spiritual formation.

Take a moment and draw two lines. One vertical and the other horizontal, making a cross. On the vertical line at the top, write the word *Thinker*, and on the bottom, write the word *Feeler*. On the horizontal line on the left, write the word *Certainty*, and on the right, write the word *Mystery*.

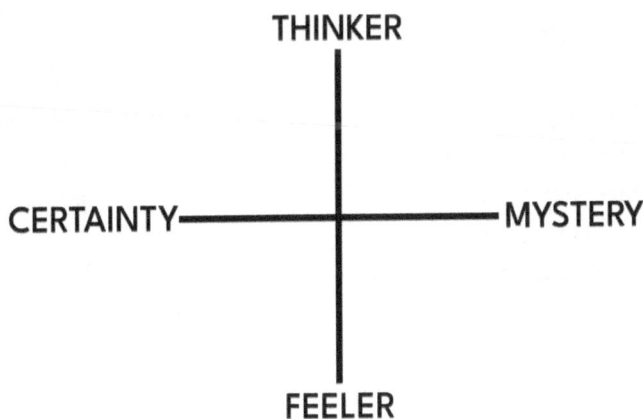

Let's define these terms you wrote down:

A. THINKER/FEELER

THINKER: The things I know in my mind
FEELER: The things I feel, that I experience,
the things down in my gut

The *thinker* is more fact-oriented rather than feeling-oriented. The thinkers can sometimes get annoyed with the feelers. The *feeler* is less concerned with facts and more concerned with his or her feelings. The feelers sometimes get annoyed with the thinkers because they don't trust their guts. Now, let's assess what direction on the line that you lean. On this vertical line, put a dot between thinker and feeler where you think you land.

Now let's discuss the horizontal line and the other two terms.

B. CERTAINTY/MYSTERY

CERTAINTY: The things that I know that I know
MYSTERY: The things that I know that I don't
know, the things that I know I can't know

First, let's talk about this word *certainty* on the left side. These are more of the logical people. These are the people who like to analyze. They don't tend to make many decisions without having the proper time to analyze them so they can have assurance that they have made the right decision. Extreme certainty people can sometimes experience what I call the paralysis of analysis. They are afraid of making the wrong decision without having all the facts.

And then on the right side of the line are the mystery people. These are the gamblers. These are the people who love going to the casino. "Could it be black? Could it be red? I don't know. I could win. I could lose. Who knows? It's a mystery, and I'm loving it."

These are more philosophical people. Do you lean more certainty or lean more mystery?

On this horizontal line, put a dot between certainty and mystery where you think you land.

Now let's put these things together.

Depending on which direction you lean with these two lines, you will land in one of the four quadrants. I will refer to these quadrants as cylinders. You're going to land, depending on the pair that you have chosen, in one of these four cylinders. These four cylinders correlate with the four areas of our lives mentioned by Jesus in the Gospel of Mark.

Depending on how you lean as a person, one of these four areas will be easier for you to practice. It is going to be easier for you to love God and give God your all in that cylinder because it's just more of who you are. But the other three cylinders might be a little bit more difficult for you. But remember, Jesus is calling us to love God with our *all* in *all*. Not just one cylinder but *all* four cylinders.

A Breakdown of the Four Cylinders

1. Thinker/Certainty (Theologian)

The thinker, mixed with certainty, is a recipe for someone to have a strong love for theology. This person loves to soak in all the knowledge they can get when it comes to understanding God and Scripture. This type of person is passionate about Bible study. They want to have all the questions answered so they can give a defense to anyone who asks.

The negative part of this type of person is they can become judgmental toward others who they feel don't know as much as they do. This person can have a propensity to criticize others who are less knowledgeable of the Bible than they are. This person can also tend to be so focused on being a learner of the Scriptures that they fail to live out the Scriptures in their day-to-day lives.

POSITIVE: You have strong theology and a deep hunger to learn about God and his word.

NEGATIVE: You can become judgmental toward others who may not know as much as you do. It can also cause a failure to apply the things you have learned.

This is the cylinder of loving God with your mind.

2. Certainty/Feeler (Worshipper)

The feeler, mixed with certainty, makes for a very passionate worshipper. This type of person has an easier time feeling the presence of God. Worship is this person's favorite part of a church gathering. This person will be more expressive in his or her worship and will be more prone to having tears during moments of prayer.

The tendency of this type of person is to rely too much on feelings and potentially misjudge their own relationship with God based on how they feel.

POSITIVE: You are passionate about God and all he has done for your life.

NEGATIVE: You can be too attached to your feelings and mistakenly use your feelings as a barometer of your spiritual health.

This is the cylinder of loving God with your heart.

3. Mystery/Feeler (Prayer Warrior)

The feeler, mixed with mystery, makes for a great prayer intercessor. This type of person loves to pray and be still before God. One of the best places for this type of person to connect with God is to be in a place by themself. People don't necessarily annoy them. They just simply feel closer to God when there is quiet and stillness around them.

This type of person needs to be careful not to detach themself too much from people and unintentionally move his or her life from solitude to isolation. Monks are a good example of this. They move themselves away from any interaction with people to practice being closer to God. Nowhere in the Scriptures does it tell us to live a life of isolation to be closer to God. Scripture tells us the exact opposite:

> The LORD God said, "It is not good for the man to be alone." (GENESIS 2:18 NIV)

> POSITIVE: You have a solid inner life with God. You have a high value for prayer and connecting with God personally.

> NEGATIVE: You can pull yourself away from other believers and feel you don't need anyone else in your life.

This is the cylinder of loving God with your soul.

4. Mystery/Thinker (Activist)

The thinker, mixed with mystery, makes for a person who loves action and getting things done. It is so life-giving for them to help others in need. When they see a need, they spring into action. They love to volunteer their time when they know they are helping make a difference for others.

The propensity of this type of person is they can be prone to viewing God's love for them as conditional through this framework of good deeds. For example, if they do a lot of good deeds, they can feel God is proud of them and, therefore, really loves them. If they haven't done enough good deeds, they can feel God is upset at them. They assess their relationship with God based on how much they do for God instead of how much God has done for them.

> POSITIVE: You are a doer. You get things done. You love social action. You love rolling up your sleeves and serving others.

> NEGATIVE: You can fall into a trap of believing your godliness is based on what you do for God instead of what Christ has done for you. You can mistakenly believe if you do enough good deeds, you are right with God, but if you don't do enough, he is mad at you.

This is the cylinder of loving God with your strength.

NOW THAT I have walked you through each of the four cylinders, I hope you can clearly see one of the four cylinders comes pretty naturally for you. I will refer to it as your dominant cylinder. And more than likely, if you are already a follower of Jesus, you are probably doing pretty well with loving God with that cylinder. But the real question is, how is it going with the other three?

In the following sections, I want to spend time looking at each one of these cylinders. As we look at each one of them, my prayer for you, and honestly the purpose of this entire book, is for you to discover ways you can move from loving God with your *some* to loving God with your *all* on *all* four cylinders.

> REMEMBER: Jesus goes on record to say this is the *greatest of all time* commandment.

All the other six-hundred-plus commandments can be summarized in this one.

Get this one down, and all the others will fall into place.

Think about it.

- When you love God with *all* of your mind, you are being renewed *mentally*.
- When you love God with *all* of your heart, you are being healed *emotionally*.
- When you love God with *all* of your soul, you are being transformed *spiritually*.
- When you love God with *all* of your strength, you are being activated *physically*.

If you get this one commandment down and really love God with your *all*, the door is going to be unlocked to the promises of God for your life.

One of the most inspiring quotes for me about this concept of the all factor comes from an evangelist and preacher in the nineteenth century named D. L. Moody:

> The world has yet to see what God can do with a man
> fully consecrated to him. And by God's help, I aim to
> be that man.[2]

The aim is to live a life full of love for God.

It doesn't mean you're going to hit the bull's-eye every time and live it perfectly.

You're not called to live a perfect life. You're called to live a surrendered life so that Jesus can be the manager of your life and lead you through it.

Your aim and my aim, as followers of Jesus, is to love God with our *all*.

Not halfway.

Not part-time.

Not lukewarm.

Aim for the *all*!

DISCUSSION QUESTIONS
FOR THE INTRODUCTION

The Greatest of All Time

- How do you interpret the call to love God with your *all* in each of the four areas: heart, soul, mind, and strength? Can you share examples from your own life where you feel you have succeeded or struggled in these areas?

- Caleb is highlighted as a model of following God with his *all*. What qualities do you admire in Caleb's faith, and how can you apply those qualities to your own life?

- What lessons can we learn from King Amaziah's story about the dangers of being *halfhearted* in our faith? How can this apply to our own lives today?

- How does the analogy of a four-cylinder motor help you understand your spiritual life? Are there areas where you feel like you are not firing on all cylinders, and how can you address this?

- In the self-assessment exercise regarding how we relate to God (thinker/feeler and certainty/mystery), where do you see yourself on these axes, and how does this influence your approach to loving God and others?

- Reflecting on the four cylinders (theologian, worshipper, prayer warrior, activist), which one would you say is your dominant cylinder? In what ways have you seen yourself lean into this area more than the other three areas of your faith?

- Out of the four cylinders, which one do you feel you excel best in, and which ones do you find challenging?

- What are some practical steps you can take this week to move from loving God with some to loving him with *all*?

PART 1

ALL MY SOUL

*The seat of the soul is
where the inner world and
the outer world meet.*

—JOSEPH CAMPBELL

A Hole in My Soul

AS WE BEGIN our look at each one of the cylinders for our faith, as mentioned in the *GOAT* commandment, I personally feel that the order in which they are listed is not as important as making sure they are all being implemented in our lives.

With that in mind, instead of looking at them in the order Scripture gives them to us, I want to cover each of them in the order of influence I believe they have in each of our lives. Examining these cylinders reveals how they influence one another and how each one builds off the health of the other.

- The soul influences your mind.
- The mind influences your heart.
- The heart influences your strength.

I will begin with the soul because the soul is the core of who you are. The soul is the deepest part of you. It is your spirit. Your innermost being. The soul plays a pivotal role in how your life goes. As it goes with your soul, so it goes with your life.

Most importantly, your soul is the eternal part of who you are.

Listen to Jesus comment about this reality as he is encouraging his disciples not to be afraid of the people around them:

> And do not fear those who kill the body but cannot
> kill the *soul*. Rather fear him who can destroy both
> *soul* and *body* in hell. (MATTHEW 10:28 ESV)

Your soul is the one and only part of you that you actually take with you when you die.

A doctor named Duncan MacDougall conducted a study in the early 1900s. He believed the human soul was material and, therefore, had mass. He constructed a special bed in his office "arranged on a light framework built upon very delicately balanced platform beam scales." He installed upon this bed a succession of six patients in the end stages of terminal illnesses. He observed them before, during, and after the process of death and measured any corresponding changes in weight. His results with these six patients showed a weight loss of three-fourths of an ounce, which is 21.3 grams. He did the same experiment on dogs and found no weight difference at all. His conclusion was the human soul has a weight to it.[3]

Through the last century, scientists have scoffed at this experiment. Again, it was the early 1900s, but I like it because it puts a focus on the importance of the soul. We don't really think much about the soul. It is definitely the more neglected cylinder out of the other cylinders mentioned in this *GOAT* commandment. Why do we neglect our souls so much? I believe the reason is that we don't necessarily deal with our souls on a daily basis like we do with our minds, our hearts, or our bodies.

We have already looked at the original Greek word for *all* in studying this *GOAT* commandment. Let me now introduce you to the original Greek word for *soul*:

ψυχή–*psychē* (pronounced psoo-khay').
DEFINITION: Breath—the vital force which animates the body and shows itself in breathing (basically, being alive).

Interestingly enough, the Hebrew word for *soul* is *nephesh*, and it literally means "breath." So the Bible is giving us a clue that our soul is somehow connected with our breath. According to the Hebrew Scriptures, the breath we breathe was first breathed into us by God himself:

Then the Lord God formed the man of dust from the ground, and breathed into his nostrils the breath of life; and the man became a living person. (GENESIS 2:7 NASB)

I heard one rabbi teach that the very name of God is found in our breath. Yahweh.

Take a deep breath and say the name.
(Inhale) Yahhhhhhh
(Exhale) Waaaaaaaay

Crazy! Right?
As some people say, "That'll preach."

Here is a question for you. Have you ever had the wind knocked out of you, or more accurately said, the breath knocked out of you?

I'll never forget my freshman year of high school. I decided to try out for the tackle football team. I was five foot two, and I weighed probably a hundred pounds, but I was superfast. At an early age, I had to learn to be fast because I was the youngest of six kids. I learned to run fast to prevent my siblings from being able to torture me.

I remember telling my football coach, "I'm going to be the running back because I'm fast, and those guys won't be able to tackle me." I quickly learned that I was not as fast as I thought I was. One of the first plays at a scrimmage, I was given the ball to run it outside the right tackle. I made it to the outside and saw daylight in front of me. I was running like the wind. This was when I discovered we had a linebacker on the team who was much faster than me. His two-hundred-pound body ran me down and hit me like a freight train. I was tackled so hard I believe my body made an indentation in the grass.

I remember just lying there after he got off me. I went to breathe, but nothing was there. No breath. He literally knocked the breath out of me. It is a scary feeling to have no breath.

Your soul was created to breathe. What we learn in the very next chapter after creation is this breath, this nephesh, this psychē, originally given to us from God, was knocked out of us—not by a linebacker but rather by our own rebellion.

In Genesis 3, Adam and Eve veer off course from the life God intended them to live. God gave clear instructions for how he designed them to live and how to rule in life, but they made the dreadful decision to disobey the instructions. This rebellious action caused a ripple effect, still being felt by our world to this day.

One of the dominant writers of our New Testament Scriptures is a man named Paul. In a letter he writes to his fellow Jewish believers in Rome, he describes this rebellious action using a word called *sin*:

When Adam sinned, sin entered the world. Adam's
sin brought death, so death spread to everyone, for
everyone sinned. (ROMANS 5:12 NLT)

This was the dark moment sin entered the world, and with it came
death. With the entrance of this sin came the exit of this breath.

Just like being tackled by a full-sized linebacker moving at full
speed, the nephesh, the very essence of God that made them fully alive,
was knocked out of them. And ever since that moment when sin entered the world, we've been desperately trying to get our breath back.

When your soul is missing this breath, you know intuitively something isn't quite right. It's like the Check Engine light is blinking
on the dashboard of your life.

When your strength isn't right, you can feel weak.

When your emotions aren't right, you can feel sad.

When your mind isn't right, you can feel anxious.

What are the symptoms when your soul isn't right?

Here are some common symptoms of what I like to refer to as
soul sickness:

- A SENSE OF DISCONTENTMENT WITH LIFE.
  Nothing seems to satisfy you. It's like having an itch you
  can't seem to scratch.
- A LACK OF DRIVE FOR LIVING.
  Nothing seems to be able to motivate you. Some days,
  you may even struggle to get out of bed. It may be so bad
  you sometimes think it would be better if you were no
  longer alive.
- A FEELING OF EMPTINESS.
  You have an aching void, an inner hollowness, like something is missing from your life and no amount of friendships
  with other people seem to make it go away.

- **A SENSE OF BEING LOST.**
  You are wandering through life dazed and confused with
  no clear direction of where you should be going or what
  you should be doing.

Maybe I just described how you've been feeling lately.

I believe those feelings are ways your soul is trying to get your attention that something is not right.

There are so many examples in pop culture of people who found fame and fortune, but never found fulfillment.

One person I think of is Hall of Fame football player Deion Sanders. Deion, now more popularly known as Coach Prime, has experienced success in so much of his life, most recently as the head football coach for the University of Colorado. There's an interesting fact about Deion Sanders that you may not know. He is very outspoken about his faith in Christ, but he wasn't always like that. At the height of his success as a professional football player, playing for the Dallas Cowboys, winning the Super Bowl, and also, at the same time, playing professional baseball, he found himself completely lost.

> I tried everything. Parties, women, buying expensive
> jewelry. Nothing helped. There was no peace, just
> emptiness inside. When I found Christ, I found what
> I had been missing all those years.[4]

Did you catch what he said?

None of his successes or accomplishments could fill the emptiness because what he was experiencing was soul sickness.

Without God in your life, there is a hole in your soul. He is the only one who can heal the hole and satisfy your soul.

A *protein bar* can satisfy your *strength*.

A *friend* can satisfy your *heart*.
A *podcast* can satisfy your *mind*.
But *only God* can satisfy your *soul*.

A Soul Detox

ONE OF MY favorite parables of Jesus is a parable commonly
referred to as the Parable of the Seed and the Sower. It's found
in all three synoptic Gospels. In this parable, Jesus uses a metaphor
of a farmer throwing seeds onto various types of soil. Out of the four
different soils, only the seed that fell on good soil produced a crop.
From this parable, we learn it's the soil that makes all the difference.

I think it is a fun coincidence that soil and soul are only one
letter removed from being the same word in the English language.
I believe Jesus is showing us a very important truth about our soul
through this parable.

When the soil is good, it produces something significant, something of value, something that is good. When the soil is not right,
all kinds of problems pop up.

There is a very similar effect between the soil of the ground and
the soul of a person.

When your soul is good, your life produces something significant,
something of value, something good. When your soul is not right,
well, you get the idea.

Years ago, Tara and I bought a house that had a side yard with some
really dead-looking fruit trees. There was a whole village of gophers

living in the yard that were having a feast with the area around the trees. In addition to the gopher problem, it was evident the trees weren't getting watered. I thought two of them were for sure dead. I had a few gardener friends of mine look at them, and they told me to get rid of them because they weren't going to be able to recover.

However, there was something in me, maybe it was the pastor in me who thought, *I serve a God that resurrects dead things, so I'm going to give them a chance to come back to life.* I knew if these trees were to have any kind of chance to make it, I had to address the soil problem.

I went after the gophers first. Once the gophers were removed, I was able to seal up the holes and fertilize the ground. I also started watering the soil around the trees on a regular basis. After a few months of the right ingredients and the right care, a miracle happened. The trees came back to life. The next year, these very same trees produced the most beautiful fruit. We had a whole crop of oranges, lemons, and grapefruit.

Here's my point. I am far from a horticulturist. All it took was giving the soil a much-needed makeover for it to become good. When the soil became good, the trees produced fruit.

I want you to know Jesus is the master gardener for your soul. He came to this world to restore your soul. He is the active ingredient your soul needs to become good.

He is able to break up the hard places of your soul that are there because of the hard things you have endured in this life.

He is able to remove the rocky places in your soul that are preventing you from growing deeper.

He is able to weed out the worries of this world that are choking your soul.

How does Jesus restore the soul? It is a two-step process:

1. **HANDLING THE SIN PROBLEM**
    All the rebellion in us that was responsible for knocking the

breath out of our souls in the first place must be dealt with. It was this act of rebellion that introduced the world to death. Jesus came to this world and lived a perfect, blameless life. With that perfect life came a perfect and unblemished soul. With both a perfect life and a perfect soul, Jesus died on the cross to cancel out death once and for all. His death meant the death of death. Through his death, Jesus covered our sin and shame, making it possible for us to be fully restored to God.

But this death is only half of the miracle.

2. HANDLING THE SOUL PROBLEM

After his death comes the resurrection. On the third day, Jesus came back to life.

The Gospel of John tells us that, after the resurrection, a woman named Mary, who Jesus had helped during his ministry, was crying outside the area where Jesus was buried. Jesus appeared to her and asked, "Why are you crying?" Here is the wild part of this encounter. Mary first mistakenly thought Jesus was a gardener. I don't think that mistaken identity was a coincidence. This was what I like to call a God-wink. Sin is what caused Adam and Eve to be kicked out of the garden at the beginning of creation. Now that sin has been taken care of, Jesus appears as a gardener to give us an invitation to come back into the garden life with God, where he restores our souls by filling us with his Spirit.

Jesus died to get you into heaven, but he resurrected to get heaven into you.

And let me tell you a fun fact.

The same word for *spirit* in the Greek language can also be defined as "breath." The word is *pneuma* (prounounded pen-OO-mah or pnyoo-MAH). It means "spirit," but it also means "breath" or "wind."

After Jesus was resurrected, he had a bizarre moment with his disciples:

> And with that he *breathed* on them and said, "Receive the *Holy Spirit*." (JOHN 20:22 NIV)

The disciples were huddled around Jesus, and he *breathed* on them. No one knows exactly how Jesus did this, but this action very much communicated something to them. He wanted them to connect the dots for what was about to happen to them.

Fast-forward to the believers assembled in the upper room, as written about in Acts 2. The Holy Spirit came upon them as *wind* swept into the upper room. Jesus wanted these followers to understand that the Spirit of God was going to restore their souls by giving them their *breath* back.

This is what the Spirit of God does. He restores your soul.

Your soul is healed.

Your soul is alive.

Your soul is breathing again.

This is another reason why I love Psalm 23 so much and why I believe it's the Bible's greatest hit song:

> He restores my soul. (PSALM 23:3 NASB 1995).

To restore means "to repair, renovate, or return to a former condition."

So there's a former condition that God is calling us back to where we actually are able to live with his breath breathing not just on us but breathing in us.

Since God is the one who made us, only he can restore us because only he knows what we truly need to restore our souls.

I want you to know God has designed your soul to breathe. Your soul actually craves it, and the only way your soul is going to breathe again is by allowing the breath of God to breathe back into your soul, just as he did with the first man at the beginning of creation.

It's time to let your soul breathe again.

If you are reading this and have never made a decision to give your life to God, to be forgiven of your sin, and to be filled with his Spirit, I think now is a great moment for you to consider it.

Here is how to experience a restored soul:

1. Recognize your soul is empty, and nothing can fill it but God himself.
2. Believe Jesus died for you to be forgiven and restored back into a relationship with God.
3. Surrender your life to Jesus and invite him to become the master gardener of your soul.
4. Ask the Spirit of God to fill your soul and take over your life.

Once you do this, the emptiness of your soul will be filled, and the gardening of your soul will begin.

Good soil produces good results.

A good soul also produces good results.

The end of Psalm 23 gives us a great picture of the results of a person with a restored soul:

> Surely your goodness and love will follow me all the days of my life, and I will dwell in the house of the Lord forever. (PSALM 23:6 NIV)

Loving God with All Your Soul

Remember, the *GOAT* commandment of God is to love him with *all* of your soul.

Not with some.

Not with part.

But with your *all*.

How do you love God with *all* of your soul?

I believe Jesus gives us the answer in another passage of Scripture:

> Come to me, all you who are weary and burdened, and
> I will give you rest. Take my yoke upon you and learn
> from me, for I am gentle and humble in heart, and
> you will find rest for your souls. (MATTHEW 11:28–30 NIV)

The Greek word used for the word *rest* in this passage can also be translated as the word *refreshment*.

Let me paraphrase what Jesus is telling all of us through this passage:

"Hey, if you feel exhausted, if you feel worn out, come to me. Yoke up with me and learn my ways. If you do, you are going to find refreshment for your soul."

You will find *refreshment* for your *psychē*.

You will find refreshment for your souls so that you can be fully alive and live life, live purpose, and live the promise that God wants for your life.

What do you typically do when you feel exhausted and worn out in life?

When you are worn out, this world offers several options for you to cope with your exhaustion.

You might turn to food.

You might turn to television.

You might turn to a drink.

You might turn to a pill.

What you need to know is the food, the entertainment, the drink, the pill—they all may temporarily numb you, but they aren't going to be able to satisfy your soul, and in some cases, they may actually damage your life.

So the very thing you're trying to do, trying to find rest for your life, is only going to be found in finding rest for your soul.

And the only way you're going to find rest for your soul is getting the breath of God back into that soul. That's how you do it.

In this instruction, Jesus is letting us know when we come to him and connect with him, he puts breath back into our souls. How do you love God with *all* of your soul?

Step One: Come to Jesus

YOU HAVE TO come to Jesus.

Have you heard this expression before in a conversation with someone? "We had our *come-to-Jesus* moment." What does that mean? It means we had to have a serious convo.

Coming to Jesus means so much more than praying a prayer to receive him as your Lord and Savior. That prayer is important, but that is by no means what Jesus is talking about in this passage.

What Jesus is teaching in this passage is not a one-and-done *come-to-Jesus* moment. He is inviting you and me into a way of life, a way of life where we sit with him to be with him on a regular basis.

Why don't we do this? Why don't we turn to Jesus more? Why don't we come to him more?

I have a few ideas why we don't:

1. **WE THINK WE CAN HANDLE THINGS ON OUR OWN.**
    We don't need to get God involved in all the details.

2. **WE OFTEN FORGET WHAT GOD IS REALLY LIKE.**
    We forget God is a loving Father who cares for us like a father
    cares for a small child. God isn't going to scold you when you
    come to him for rest and refreshment. He's going to love you.
    But you've got to come to him. That's the first step.

Making Time for Jesus

The challenge with regularly coming to Jesus is there are so many
things these days bidding for your time. It can make it very difficult
for you to have the time to do it.

In my twenties, I learned that life is fast. My wife, Tara, and I
started having babies in our twenties, and I learned really quickly
that the schedule was full. And if I didn't intentionally make time
to come to Jesus, I wasn't going to come to Jesus.

Most everyone I know who has a relationship with Jesus has a
desire to come to Jesus. The desire is not the problem. It is the priority that is the problem. You wake up late and hurry off to work,
thinking you will wake up early and spend time with God tomor-
row. The day slips away from you, and a day turns into a week. A
week turns into a month. A month turns into a year. Time seems
to move faster and faster the older you get.

The saving grace is you're able to attend a Sunday gathering.

Obviously as a pastor, I am a big advocate for you attending a
weekend gathering. However, this should not be your only FaceTime
with Jesus for the week. Attending a weekend gathering should
be the grand finale of lots of FaceTime you have had with Jesus
all week. I believe a weekend gathering should be filled more with
confirmation than information, confirming things He has been
saying to you all week in the personal time you have been having.

Can you imagine what kind of physical shape you would be in if you only fed your body once a week? Eating once a week is not going to give you the nourishment to get you through your week. You have to be nourishing yourself daily. Some people need to eat every couple of hours. If you ignore your body and refuse to eat, your stomach will start yelling at you. It's crazy how much noise the stomach can make and how loud it can be, especially in a quiet meeting at work.

I am convinced the soul has its own way of making noise when it's neglected. There is a darkness that seeps in and surrounds you. Your soul is keenly aware of it, and you will start feeling it just like you hear your stomach yell at you when you neglect to feed it.

If you are going to be victorious in loving God with *all* of your soul, it starts with you making the time to come to him. Be serious about it. Set it up on your calendar like you would if you were scheduling an important meeting with a business client.

As a young adult with a wife and babies, my special time with Jesus was early in the morning. I called it *Breakfast with Jesus*. It was the only time that I knew I wouldn't be interrupted. I love doing this at the beginning of the day because it's not like I put in ten minutes and I'm done (like some kind of hyper cardio workout). I treat my morning time with Jesus as an opener. This is the time when I FaceTime heaven and begin a call that I stay connected on for the entire day.

Do you think connecting with Jesus in the morning like this would make a difference in how you handle your day?

- How you deal with other coworkers?
- How you deal with your family?
- How you deal with your own mental stressors?

Of course, it will make a difference.

I want to end this point by telling you a bizarre God story I had in one of my early morning *Breakfast with Jesus* sessions.

As I was spending time with the Lord early in the morning in my downstairs living room, it was quiet. All my family was still in bed sleeping. Very often as I am sitting with Jesus, I will have thought bubbles hit me. They aren't audible voices, but they are very strong internal thoughts. I heard clearly, "Death Cab for Cutie." It was such a strange phrase. I kept hearing it repeat in my mind. I wrote it down in my personal journal. A little while after this happened, my oldest daughter, Kylee, came downstairs. I said, "Kylee, have you ever heard the phrase 'Death Cab for Cutie'?" She said, "I think it's a band."

I am being completely truthful with you when I say this. I had no idea this was a band. Maybe my subconscious had heard this before, but I honestly had no idea there was a band by the name of Death Cab for Cutie.[5] I went right to my laptop and googled the name, and sure enough, there was the band. I clicked the first link I saw for the band, and it took me to one of their YouTube music videos called "I Will Possess Your Heart."

After a very long instrumental intro, the lyrics started flowing. In the song, the lyricist wants the person they are talking with to see the incredible potential they have in their relationship together, but the only way for the relationship to reach that potential is by spending time together. By spending time together, the lyricist proclaims the title of the song, "I Will Possess Your Heart."[6]

I don't know much about this band. I don't believe they are a Christian band, but I heard God speak to me so clearly through these lyrics.

There is a reason so many miracles happened through the apostles and early followers of Jesus. They watched Jesus spend so much time with his heavenly Father. They knew the power was rooted in the relationship with God, not in themselves.

What a *wow* moment!

God showed me the power of *coming to him* while I was in the middle of *coming to him*.

I left my house shortly after that moment for an appointment I had with a couple in our church. I thought the appointment was for marriage counseling, but it turns out they wanted to meet with me because they both had a vision of creating a 24-7 prayer room at the church.

The irony of this meeting is that they were inspired to do this from a book my friend had found in my garage when he was helping me clean it up a few months before this meeting. Long story short, I told this couple the God story with the song that had just happened, and three months later, we started a forty-day, 24-7 prayer room.

God did so many powerful things for people in those forty days. We saw marriages restored. We saw people healed of illness. We saw people come back to God. It revived our church.

When you *come to Jesus*, powerful things take place.

Just as the *Death Cab for Cutie* song suggests, if you want to reach your full potential of God moving in your life, you have to spend time with Jesus.

Step Two: Connect with Jesus

THE SECOND PART of finding rest for your soul is what I refer to as connecting with him. This is the taking of his yoke.

In Jewish tradition, a *yoke* refers to a rabbi's specific interpretation and application of the law, essentially meaning that when a student followed a rabbi, they were *under the yoke* of that rabbi's teachings, adhering to their particular understanding of the Scriptures and practices. The *yoke* was also a piece of wood that was used to put two cattle together to pull a cart or plow a field. Its purpose was to make a load easier because the two cattle were sharing it together.

Jesus wants you to *yoke* up with him. The *yoke* is a symbol of partnership. Jesus wants to come alongside you and help you with the weightiness of all that you are carrying.

When you're yoked with Jesus, you move together with him. You move in the same direction and at the same speed. I might add you move in the *right* direction and at the *right* speed, all while moving with a *lighter* load.

When you are yoked up with Jesus, you are declaring, "I'm doing this day with Jesus. It's me and him." That's connecting with him.

In the Gospel of John, chapter 15, Jesus says this:

> Abide in me, and I in you. As the branch cannot bear fruit by itself, unless it abides in the vine, neither can you, unless you abide in me. I am the vine; you are the branches. Whoever abides in me and I in him, he it is that bears much fruit, for apart from me you can do nothing. If anyone does not abide in me he is thrown away like a branch and withers; and the branches are gathered, thrown into the fire, and burned. If you abide in me, and my words abide in you, ask whatever you wish, and it will be done for you. By this my Father is glorified, that you bear much fruit and so prove to be my disciples. As the Father has loved me, so have I loved you. Abide in my love. (JOHN 15:4–9 ESV)

Some translations of this text use the word *remain* instead of *abide*. The word conveys the idea of being constantly connected.

Jesus is letting us know the more we're constantly and consistently in this connection with him, the more we will see his goodness sprouting from our lives.

The more you're connected with Jesus, the more his Spirit is infiltrating your life. His Spirit is the active ingredient that gives you good soil to bring you good fruit.

The more of his Spirit you have moving in your life, the more powerful results you will see coming from your life.

The question I had when I was still pretty young in my faith was, "How do I stay connected with him in the midst of all my other daily tasks?"

I had someone recommend a book to me called *The Practice of the Presence of God* by Brother Lawrence, a seventeenth-century monk. The book is actually a collection of letters he had written in which he highlighted the need to remind ourselves that God is with us continually, even in the smallest of chores and duties. In one of his entries, he writes, "My most normal habit is to simply keep my attention on God, and to be generally and lovingly aware of Him."[7]

The best way to practice this kind of soul care for yourself is to have some reminders set throughout the day to help you continue to stay connected with God. I call these *touchpoints*. A *touchpoint* is anything that brings you close to Jesus and causes you to have an awareness of his "thereness" for your life.

The ancient practice of communion, or as some people refer to it as *the Eucharist*, is a practice to help believers with this idea of continuing to stay connected with Jesus.

At the Last Supper, on the eve of his arrest, Jesus took both bread and wine from the dinner table and told his disciples, "As often as you eat and drink, do this in remembrance of me."[8] This is where the practice of communion originated.

Every time you take these elements of communion, you recognize and remember the body of Jesus, which was broken for you to make you whole again. You're recognizing and remembering the blood of Jesus that was spilled for you to cleanse you and give you life again.

Some people only take communion every once in a while, but if we take Jesus at his word, we ought to remember him every time we eat, which for most of us is at least three times a day. That's a good start to help you stay connected with him throughout the day.

Another practice that helps me stay connected with Jesus throughout a busy day is driving with the radio off in my car. Every time I get in my car to drive, which is quite frequent, the silence becomes an invitation for me to bring God into that moment.

Maybe for you, it could be leaving sticky notes in different places around your home and your office, or maybe it could be your phone changing screensavers every hour with different Bible verses.

Find some way to give yourself touchpoints so you stay constantly connected with Jesus throughout your busy day.

Step Three: Learn from Jesus

THE THIRD PART of finding rest for your soul is learning from him. This is a declaration.

"Jesus, I'm positioning myself not just to be connected with you, but to also learn from you, to follow your lead for how to live my life."

Learning from Jesus involves using his life as a standard for how we should be living ours. I find myself auditing my life all the time in how I am living compared to the way Jesus lived.

There are a lot of attributes we can learn from Jesus, but in this text, Jesus features two very significant ones:

ALL MY SOUL

57

"For I am gentle and humble in heart."

Two of the greatest soul refreshing ways of Jesus is his gentleness and humility.

He modeled gentleness and humility in everything he did.

Let's take a soul audit right now.

Have you been gentle this week?

Have you been humble this week?

It's probably good to mention what being humble looks like. Humility is lowering yourself so that you can elevate others. Have you been doing a good job with lowering yourself so you can elevate others?

I want to be very cautious on this point. Jesus is not wanting us to compile a list of his ways and beat ourselves up trying to live out all his attributes. So many religions have done this. That is not what I would call refreshing for the soul. I would call it draining for the soul.

There was a trend in church culture back in the '90s where people wore bracelets stamped with the letters WWJD. These letters stood for *What would Jesus do?* The point of the bracelet was to remind the person wearing the bracelet to make better decisions for his or her life, the kind of decisions Jesus would make for his life. (I think I still have a few of these bracelets tucked away in a drawer somewhere, along with some compact discs.)

The concept of trying to live as Jesus lived is good, but it can also cause your relationship with God to become a bit distorted. Your relationship with God is based on his love toward you, on what he has done for you. It's not based on what you do for him. His loyal love and faithfulness toward you is what makes your relationship with him possible.

You have to always remember you are not learning the ways of Jesus to earn more favor with Jesus. You are learning from him so you can find rest for your soul.

The great news for us is we have some heavenly help to assist us in *learning from Jesus*. Scripture teaches us the most effective way we can learn from him is by letting the Holy Spirit breathe into us.

In John 14, Jesus says the Spirit who is our helper will teach you all things:

> But the Advocate, the Holy Spirit, whom the Father will send in my name, will teach you all things and will remind you of everything I have said to you. (JOHN 14:26 NIV)

The early church saw the Holy Spirit as part of the Godhead. The word *trinity* is not in the Bible, but the term was created by early church fathers to try to explain the way God works within three distinct roles.

I love this explanation of the Trinity from gotquestions.org:

> As all orthodox Christians agree, the doctrine of the Trinity holds that God is one essence but three distinct persons; God has one nature, but three centers of consciousness; God is only one What, but three Whos. (GOTQUESTIONS.ORG)[9]

All that to say, the Holy Spirit plays a very important role in your life and your faith.

Through the Holy Spirit living in you, you have a constant helper, you have a constant teacher, you have a constant counselor, you have a constant guide. Through the Holy Spirit living in you, you will be constantly *learning from Jesus*.

I love this excerpt from the late Billy Graham from his book entitled *The Holy Spirit* about the role of the Holy Spirit in a believer's life. "If we are to live a life of sanity in our modern world, if we wish to be men and women who can live victoriously, we need this two-sided gift God has offered us: first, the work of the *Son* of God *for us*; second, the work of the *Spirit* of God *in us*. In this way, God has answered mankind's two great cries: the cry for *forgiveness* and the cry for *goodness*."[10]

I need Jesus for my *eternal* life.

I need the Holy Spirit for my *internal* life.

Scripture shows us clearly the difference the Holy Spirit makes on believers by documenting the massive difference in the believers before and after the Holy Spirit was given to them.

The Holy Spirit is trying to teach you things this week.

Maybe it's in the form of you being convicted of some poor behavior you committed in front of some coworkers.

Maybe it's in the form of a word you keep hearing repeatedly while you are in prayer, saying to you, "It's not my will for you. That's not the direction I've called you."

Or perhaps it's through reading the Bible, and as you are reading a verse, the Spirit highlights the verse, and you have an overwhelming sensation, "That verse is for me today."

How do you love God with *all* of your soul?

You come to Jesus.

You connect with Jesus.

You learn from Jesus.

Jesus is giving us the secret sauce to experience soul refreshment in our lives.

This is authentic soul care.

How do you care for your soul?

You love God with it.

All of it.

The Tale of Two Sisters

As Jesus and his disciples were on their way, he came to a village where a woman named Martha opened her home to him. She had a sister called Mary, who sat at the Lord's feet listening to what he said. But Martha was distracted by all the preparations that had to be made. She came to him and asked, "Lord, don't you care that my sister has left me to do the work by myself? Tell her to help me!" "Martha, Martha," the Lord answered, "you are worried and upset about many things, but few things are needed—or indeed only one. Mary has chosen what is better, and it will not be taken away from her."
(LUKE 10:38–42 NIV)

TWO SISTERS WERE having a dinner party for Jesus and some of their friends. Their names were Martha and Mary. Martha was getting the dinner party ready. She was in the kitchen. The disciples were gathered around Jesus as he taught them in the living room. And Mary, her sister, was crashing the disciples' little Bible study. She wasn't really crashing. Jesus wanted her there. Martha is appalled by this and decides to get Jesus involved. "Jesus, I need help in the kitchen. Get on to Mary and tell her to come and help me." To Martha's surprise, Jesus doesn't get on to Mary but instead corrects Martha. Jesus told her, "Martha, you're doing a lot of things, but there's only one thing that's really important, and your sister has found it."

What we learn from this tale of two sisters is that ministry to the Lord is so much more important than ministry for the Lord.

Sitting at the feet of Jesus is the most powerful thing you can do to love the Lord with all your soul.

I want you to know God has a *dominant* love language—it is *quality time.*

When you're sitting at the feet of Jesus, you are absorbing the breath of God, the very essence of the Spirit of God that your soul requires to be fully alive and healthy.

It turns out this cylinder of the soul, for this *GOAT* commandment, holds the greatest importance. Why? It turns out the soul is the operating center for all the other cylinders. When your soul is full of God, it's way easier for your mind to be right, for your heart to be right, and for your strength to be right.

The Powerful Practice of Prayer

THE BIGGEST WAY you come to Jesus, connect with Jesus, and learn from Jesus is through the practice of prayer.

You may have a deep understanding of prayer, but in the post-Christian era we are all now living in, I feel a good recap of what prayer is and what prayer is not would be good for your soul. Prayer is super simple, and in my experience, most people overthink it. Prayer can be simply defined as engaging in a conversation with God, where you both talk and listen, much like you would with another person.

I like to say it this way. Prayer is a dialogue, not a monologue. Prayer is where you speak to God, but it is also where God speaks to you.

Maybe the reason you don't pray is because you really don't know how to pray, and you're making it more difficult than it really needs to be.

The disciples observed a rhythm to the way Jesus lived his life:

> But Jesus often withdrew to lonely places and prayed.
> (LUKE 5:16 NIV)

Not only did they observe a rhythm, but also they witnessed powerful results. Miracles were happening all around Jesus, and the disciples saw how it all traced back to his practice of prayer.

The disciples were so convinced that the miracles were connected to his prayer time that they asked Jesus to teach them how to pray. They all knew what prayer was, but Jesus was modeling a prayer life that was producing powerful results. What they were asking Jesus was, "Teach us to pray in the same way you pray so we can experience the same results you have."

Jesus did give the disciples a pattern of prayer. (You can find this pattern of prayer in Matthew 6 and Luke 11.) Most people commonly refer to this prayer as *the Lord's Prayer.* Some people go as far as to memorize this prayer, but I want you to know the power isn't in the exact words of this prayer Jesus teaches. Memorizing Scripture will always be a good thing for you to do, but it is not going to make your prayers more powerful. The power is in the connection. If you memorize words, you can easily recite them with your voice while your brain is thinking about something entirely different. So you could be praying a memorized prayer to God while you are thinking about grilling some steak for dinner tonight. That's not really connecting with God.

I look at *the Lord's Prayer* as more of an outline Jesus is teaching us to follow, making sure we cover all the power points. Through all the years I have been following Jesus, I have been introduced to some amazing prayer outlines that I have followed. I frequently change up my prayer outlines so my brain stays connected with my prayer time and not on the steak dinner.

In this book, I want to walk you through one of my favorite prayer outlines. It's called *ACTS*:

- Adoration
- Confession
- Thanksgiving
- Supplication

This is a simple outline I use to make sure I have a quality experience with God in prayer. This prayer outline covers all the bases, in my opinion, and it's super easy to remember.

Adoration

It is always a great practice to start prayer off with adoration. So every time I spend time with God intentionally, I just want to take a moment at the beginning to appreciate who God is and how big God is.

The idea here is magnifying God. And when you hear the word *magnify*, you probably think of making something bigger than what it is because that's what magnification does. But you don't make God bigger than he is. When you're giving adoration to God, you're putting God in his right size. And this is so important for your soul because, right now, this world is trying to convince you that your problems, circumstances, and situations are bigger than what you can handle. And that might be true, but they're not bigger than God.

God is always greater than your greatest problem, and when you magnify God, you minimize your trouble.

And when you start adoring God, what you're doing is you're magnifying God. You're saying, "God, you are the creator of the universe. You made all things, including me." And when you spend that moment at the beginning of your prayer time acknowledging who God is, it starts minimizing the size of your problems because you're putting your problems in the right perspective of an all-powerful God.

Confession

The second part of this pattern of prayer is confession.

Scripture teaches us an important truth:

> If we confess our sins, he is faithful and just and will forgive us our sins and purify us from all unrighteousness. (1 JOHN 1:9 NIV)

This word *confess* in the Greek language literally translates to mean "to say the same thing as."

When you're confessing something to God, it's not the same as confessing something to another person. God already sees it. God already knows it. This confession is where you come into agreement with God and speak out all the ways you know you are missing the mark of how God wants you to live. These are all the things you are doing that are not in alignment with God's will for your life.

Every day, there's probably a moment, maybe a couple of moments, when you're realizing, "Yep, I missed that one. I messed that up."

Your confession is speaking those moments out in prayer and saying, "God, I say the same thing that you say, that this is not good or healthy for my life, and I want it out of my life."

That's what real confession is.

And when you confess, you are actually purifying your life.

It's God's soul cleanser for your life.

Thanksgiving

Our culture is so good about reminding us of all the things that are wrong in our lives, all the things that we don't have in our lives. Our whole economy is built on dissatisfying you with what you have so that you will go out and buy something else. Every September, Apple rolls out its latest products. Typically, it will have a new upgraded phone with new features.

I have to make a confession as a pastor: I was the guy in 2007 who was in line at the AT&T store waiting for the new iPhone. For the first three or four years, I would go back and stand in the line so I could be one of the first to buy the latest model. Then I wised up. I realized the phone I had was pretty awesome. I didn't really need a new phone every year.

We are bombarded by commercials and ads constantly telling us what we have is not good enough. We should want something better. As a result, we focus on what we don't have. And unfortunately, the more you focus on what you *don't* have, the more discontent you are with what you *do* have in your own life.

I want you to know discontentment is the doorway to anxiety, depression, and all kinds of other problems in your life.

Then on top of that, we forget what is right in our lives because we're so focused on what's wrong. The negative always gets more attention than the positive. So, if there's something wrong, it is way overshadowing all the things that are right.

Do you know what giving thanks does? It helps highlight the things that are right and helps us remember the good things that we have.

Can you think of something that is right in your life?

Can you think of something you have in your life that is good?

> It is good to give thanks to the LORD, to sing praises to the Most High. (PSALM 92:1 NLT)

Go ahead and tell God right now, "Thank you!"

- "I thank you for providing me a home."
- "I thank you for providing me a job."
- "I thank you for my family."

Just thank him for something you *do* have, then give him some thanks for something that's *right* in your life.

- "God, I'm thankful for my health."
- "I'm thankful you are doing a great work in my marriage."
- "I'm grateful for the godly friends you have brought into my life who are there for me."

Just as discontentment is the *doorway for anxiety*, giving thanks is the *pathway to peace*.

We will talk more about this in the section about loving God with *all* your mind.

Supplication

This is where we get God involved with our problems and our situations. God has asked us to invite him into our situations so that he might partner with us to see heaven come to earth. This is where the miracles happen.

In the very beginning of our Bibles, we learn about how God set up the earth to operate. He gave us dominion to subdue the earth. In God's divine sovereignty, he gave us the authority to rule. We had that stolen from us pretty quickly by the evil one, and the earth has been going to hell ever since. Prayer is God's divine workaround to this original agreement. You might want to call it a divine loophole. When we pray, we are activating God's divine help in our situations, and when God steps in, the supernatural breaks out.

Miracles happen. Situations change. Demons flee. Mountains move. Seas split. Giants fall.

Your supplication releases heaven into your life.

Jesus said it this way:

> Ask and it will be given to you; seek and you will find; knock and the door will be opened to you. For everyone who asks receives; the one who seeks finds; and to the one who knocks, the door will be opened. (MATTHEW 7:7–8 NIV).

We won't be able to fully comprehend the complexity of how the spiritual realm works around us, but I like how the great theologian Charles Spurgeon said it:

> Whether we like it or not, asking is the rule of the kingdom. If you may have everything by asking in his name and nothing without asking, I beg you to see how absolutely vital prayer is. I've seen prayer do so many powerful things in my life.[11]

So, take some time to invite God into the situations that you're going through. It may bring a miracle for you and a breakthrough for someone else.

Driving in Circles

YEARS AGO, WHEN I was leading a church in the city of Las Vegas, God supernaturally provided us with a building. It happened to be right in the middle of the inner city of Las Vegas. It was a big miracle for our church. We had outgrown the space where we were meeting and needed something bigger. This new building was double the size, and the miracle for our church was the owner gave the building to us for free. We just had to take care of all the renovations ourselves. Eight months after the renovations started, we were able to move in and start meeting at our new location.

About a week after we moved into this new location, I pulled into the parking lot one morning. I was just sitting in my truck, thanking God for how he supernaturally gave us the building and supernaturally provided us with everything we needed to renovate it.

This is when I clearly heard this voice. It wasn't an audible voice. It was what I call a thought bubble, but it was so clear. I heard, "I've sent you here to change the atmosphere."

My first thought was it has to be God because it rhymes so well.

I can't remember if it was the same day, but it was definitely the same week, a representative from the police department stopped by to introduce herself and welcome us to the neighborhood. She was also a follower of Jesus and told me she had been praying for a church to come to the neighborhood. She let me know that the area around our new location was deemed by the police department to be one of the most crime-ridden areas in the city.

The following Sunday, I saw firsthand what she was talking about. A man pulled a gun on another man in our church parking lot after our last gathering. Over the next month, I had several of our young families come to me and let me know they weren't feeling safe at our church and felt they needed to find another church to attend. This, as you can imagine, devastated me. I started thinking this building was more of a curse than a miracle.

At that time, I happened to be reading a book called *The Circle Maker* by author and pastor Mark Batterson.[12] In the book, he talks about the legend of Honi, Ha-Ma'agel, a Jewish scholar who lived in the first century BC and is best known for drawing a circle in the sand and not budging from inside it until God answered his prayers for his people.

The book mentioned drawing a circle around something in your life where you need a miracle or a breakthrough, and keep praying until something happens.

This is where I learned the idea of PUSH:

- Pray
- Until
- Something
- Happens

I thought about our location dilemma and then thought about the word God gave me: "I've sent you here to change the atmosphere."

It was then that I decided to take this drawing-a-circle concept literally. I took a one-mile radius around our church building, and I decided to drive my prayer circle. I drove a one-mile radius around the neighborhood. I drove lap after lap around the neighborhood, and I was praying my heart out for this neighborhood. By the sixth lap, I didn't have a voice left. I was yelling at the top of my voice, "I come against every demon of hell and command you to leave this neighborhood in Jesus's name."

About a year after that drive-through prayer experience, that same representative from the police department stopped by the church to let me know that since we opened our church at that location, the crime rate in the whole neighborhood had dropped significantly. I attribute that change 100 percent to the power of God moving through my prayer and so many of our other church members praying for a breakthrough over that neighborhood. We saw God do so many miracles in the neighborhood after that drive-through prayer experience I did.

It wasn't long after that prayer experience that the public high school near our church actually allowed us to do an after-school rally on their campus. We saw tons of teenagers give their lives to Christ. We then started an outreach called Adopt-a-Block, where we went house to house asking if our neighbors needed anything. We even had an opportunity to pray with the postal worker delivering mail in the neighborhood, and he gave his life to Christ. God moved big time, but it was only after I moved myself to pray.

A friend once told me this:

- Much prayer equals much power.
- Some prayer equals some power.
- Little prayer equals little power.
- No prayer equals no power.

God has sent you here to change the atmosphere.

It's because the Spirit of God, the breath of God, is breathing not just on you, but in you. And that makes you a powerful person to do incredible things in this world.

Draw a circle (or drive a circle) and keep praying until something happens.

> The earnest prayer of a righteous person has great power and produces wonderful results. (JAMES 5:16 NLT)

- Adoration
- Confession
- Thanksgiving
- Supplication

Again, this prayer outline is one of many different outlines you can use. It just happens to be one of my personal favorites. It is a good idea to have a few prayer outlines to follow to keep things fresh and change things up in your prayer time with God.

The most important thing about prayer is not the outline you use or the pattern you follow but that you are actually coming to Jesus, connecting with Jesus, and learning from Jesus.

Your life can be pitiful or powerful. What makes the difference is coming into the place where the Spirit of God, the breath of God, the psychē, the nephesh, fills your being and satisfies your soul.

Prayer is the place where God breathes into your soul and fills you with his Spirit.

Prayer is the place where you love God with *all* of your *soul*.

DISCUSSION QUESTIONS FOR PART 1

All My Soul

- What does it mean to have "a hole in your soul," and how can you identify it in your own life?

- Reflect on the symptoms of soul sickness described in the chapter. Have you experienced any of these symptoms? How did they manifest in your life?

- The chapter draws a parallel between soil and soul. How can you cultivate good soil in your life to ensure your soul flourishes? What actions might you take?

- In what ways can you implement a soul detox in your daily routine?

- Consider the tale of the two sisters. What lessons about priorities can you draw from their story?

- Which aspect of the ACTS pattern of prayer do you find most challenging and why?

- How have you experienced prayer helping you in your relationship with God? Share a specific example of a powerful moment in prayer.

- Have you ever circled something in prayer and continued to pray until something happened?

PART 2

ALL MY MIND

You are who you are and what you are because of what has gone into your mind. You can change who you are and what you are by changing what goes into your mind.

—ZIG ZIGLAR

N OW THAT YOU have learned what it looks like to love God with *all* of your soul, I believe the next cylinder of importance is loving God with *all* of your mind.

The first thing you probably think about in loving God with *all* of your mind is learning and getting more knowledgeable about God.

After all, many sociologists have branded this age as the age of information.

We're continuously consuming more and more information, becoming more and more knowledgeable about all kinds of different subjects.

Thanks to the internet, AI, and the likes of Alexa and Siri, we are able to know just about anything about anything.

I have developed a habit over the last couple of years of looking up random facts about movies and shows while watching them with my wife. I know the current ages of so many actors, who are still alive, who have passed on, the city where the movie was filmed, and in some cases, the exact address of the filming location. If you are wondering where the Tanner family home is located that is featured in the opening credits for the shows *Full House* and *Fuller House*, you can find it at 1709 Broderick Street in San Francisco, California. I can map you there. Honestly, I can't help myself.

Having so much access to information is not necessarily a bad thing, as long as the information is true. And just because it's on the internet doesn't mean it's true. I think we all learned that over the last couple of years.

In many cases, having access to so much information is

superhelpful. I have saved myself quite a bit of money learning how to fix and repair stuff by watching a video on YouTube. My friends have done the same thing. We call these tutorial videos YouTube University. (Make sure to like and subscribe.)

To add even more to our knowledge base, we now have podcasts. There's literally a podcast about everything.

Then there are still old-school books like this one. It's crazy to think there was a time when Amazon existed for the sole purpose of selling books.

The question for all of us is this. With such easy access to so much knowledge, how are we using it to love God with our minds?

Here is the reality for so many of us:

We know more facts about sports teams than we do about the Bible.

We know more about politicians and their policies than we know about the matters God is most concerned with.

We know more about Hollywood gossip, who's with so and so and who broke up with so and so, than we know about the Holy Spirit and the role he is to play in our faith.

Leveling up on your knowledge of God and the Bible is for sure part of loving God with your mind, and we will be thoroughly covering some practical ways to do this in this section, but knowledge alone doesn't address loving God with *all* of your mind.

There is an even greater matter when it comes to talking about your gray matter. (See what I did there?)

Your thought life.

I am talking about those thoughts that are swimming around in your head. I like to refer to them as *thought bubbles*.

Remember the cartoon strips where the little bubble is just to the left of the character's brain? These bubbles represent the inner voice floating around in the mind but never heard audibly by anyone.

Neuroscience researchers believe we experience anywhere from six thousand to seventy thousand of these *thought bubbles* each day.[13]

Imagine if science created a way to tap into your brain and take these private *thought bubbles* and display them on a monitor screen for everyone around you to read your thoughts. That would be one scary invention. Why? Let's be honest. Even the godliest people, yes, even pastors, can have some wild *thought bubbles* pop into their minds.

Whether you're on the lower end of the spectrum, experiencing six thousand of these *thought bubbles* per day, or if you're on the upper end, experiencing seventy thousand per day, you cannot love God with *all* your mind without addressing your thought life.

Mind Wars

THERE IS A verse in the New Testament Scriptures that really shows just how important this topic of the mind is, especially when it comes to how you think:

> Therefore, prepare your minds for action, keep so-
> ber in spirit, set your hope completely on the grace
> to be brought to you at the revelation of Jesus Christ.
> (1 PETER 1:13 NASB)

The word *prepare* in the Greek language is another way of saying, "Roll up your sleeves."

This is fighter language.

I don't know how you personally feel about fighting, but this verse declares to us that there is a war going on in all our minds, so we better be ready to fight.

This is a war you can't avoid because everywhere you go, there you are. Everywhere you go, there's your thought life connected directly to you.

Here is what makes this fight so important.

Whoever wins this war of your mind also wins your heart and strength as well.

> Temptation comes from our own desires, which entice us and drag us away. These desires give birth to sinful actions. And when sin is allowed to grow, it gives birth to death. (JAMES 1:14–15 NLT)

It starts with temptation.

Have you ever thought about where temptation comes from?

Temptation always begins with a thought. It begins in the mind. You start having thoughts, and as those thoughts increase, they turn into real desires. When those desires continue to grow, you eventually pull the trigger on making ungodly choices for your life that ultimately damage your life.

How it goes with your mind determines how it goes with your heart.

How it goes with your heart determines how it goes with your strength.

Here's the chain reaction:

- Thoughts produce desires.
- Desires produce actions.
- Actions produce habits.
- Habits produce character.

This is why the war in your mind is the most important fight of your life.

Brainstorming

NEUROSCIENCE HAS DISCOVERED so much about our brains over the last few decades. One of the biggest breakthrough discoveries is how our brains process thoughts. Our brains use this system that neuroscientists refer to as neural pathways.

Neural pathways are the connections between neurons that light up when you think of something. The more you have the same recurring thought, the deeper the neural pathway becomes, meaning it will be easier and more likely for you to have that thought again in the future.

My wife and I live in an area that has lots of walking and hiking trails. Whenever we go out walking or hiking, we never struggle to find the trail. It's easy to identify because the ground has been walked on so much: There is no grass or brush on the path, only hard-pressed dirt. This is the same way our brains operate when it comes to pathways of thought. The more established and walked on a pathway is, the more likely your thoughts will take that pathway again. These pathways are also referred to as patterns of thought.

If you don't like the way you think, I have good news for you. It's actually possible to change it.

In many recent studies conducted on the brain and neural pathways, neuroscience has discovered that it is possible to change your thought patterns by introducing your brain to new thoughts. The scientific term for this is called *neuroplasticity*. According to the National Library of Medicine, "neuroplasticity is the ability of the nervous system to change its activity in response to intrinsic or extrinsic stimuli by reorganizing its structure, functions, or connections."[14] This scientific discovery has led to breakthrough techniques to help people recover from brain injuries and severe traumatic experiences.

I love it when science catches up with what Scripture has been saying for thousands of years.

> Do not conform to the pattern of this world, but be transformed by the renewing of your mind. Then you will be able to test and approve what God's will is—his good, pleasing and perfect will. (ROMANS 12:2 NIV)

You are *transformed* by the renewing of your mind.

Transformed is a powerful word. The word is *metamorphoō* in the original Greek language. In the English language, it's the word *metamorphosis*. It's the word we use to describe when a caterpillar becomes a butterfly or when a tadpole becomes a bullfrog.

When your mind is renewed, there is a literal change that takes place from who you used to be into who God has called you to be.

This Scripture declares to us that life change takes place when our minds get renewed.

In some translations, the word *renovated* is used instead of the word *renewed*. I like using the word *renovated* because it really gives us a visual image of what needs to happen in order for us to be changed. There has to be a renovation of the mind.

The first step of any renovation project is what Chip Gaines of the show *Fixer Upper* calls "Demo Day."

In order to build the new, you have to demo the old.

The old patterns of thinking are really what many people find the most difficult to overcome.

Let's be honest: As we have lived our lives, we've picked up a lot of negative thoughts. Multiple sources I have read about this phenomenon of negative thinking have said that up to 80 percent of our thought life is negative in nature. As I think about my own thought life, this may be an accurate number.

I like to call this *stinkin' thinkin'*.

Maybe for you, the *stinkin' thinkin'* can be traced back all the way to childhood and words you endured from abusive people in your life. One negative word spoken to you during your formative years can stick with you for the rest of your life. These negative words can play over and over in your mind like a song on repeat.

Whoever made up the rhyme "Sticks and stones may break my bones, but words will never hurt me" got it way wrong.

Maybe for you, the *stinkin' thinkin'* stems from your adolescence when you made foolish and unwise decisions that have had a lasting effect on your life. These are primarily negative thoughts of regret. Maybe the old patterns of thinking are actually from current adult issues you are facing, where you feel stuck in a terrible pit rather than just being on a negative pathway. Addictions can be a great example of this, whether it's food, drugs, alcohol, or porn.

If you are like me, don't you feel these negative thought bubbles get amplified sometimes? It's almost like the only voice you can hear in your head is dark and certainly isn't helpful for you.

I like to think of the mind as having a tiny stage with a mic on a stand, and every day, there is an open mic performance happening in your head.

There is a competition going on right now in your mind of who is going to take the stage and get to be the voice on the mic.

When I was a youth pastor back in the late '90s, I would bring our youth to this huge Christian music festival up in Northern California. The first year we did this, the festival was brand new, and they still had a lot of kinks to work out. That is to be expected the first time you do anything. Well, the organizers had a special VIP section at the front of this massive six-foot-tall stage. This VIP section was separated from the rest of the general ticket holders by only this thin orange construction fencing you can buy at any hardware store. All the great bands were there that year, including one of my personal favorites, Newsboys. After about the sixth song in the Newsboys set, the crowd of fifty thousand people had pushed over the VIP fencing. Because the Newsboys were one of my favorite bands, I was right up front against the stage with some of my youth.

When Newsboys started their song "Breakfast," I noticed a girl had climbed the six-foot stage somehow and was joining one of the band members on the mic to sing with him. I looked at my youth group around me to laugh about this, and one of my students held his hands out, offering me a boost to get up on the stage as well. Being the model youth pastor I was, I used his boost to launch me onto the stage. The band saw me and started laughing. There were now several audience members on the stage with the band, including me. What was my first move as the newest member of the Newsboys? I went straight for the lead singer's mic, and with fifty thousand people in front of me, I said, "Hi Tara!"

My wife, who was all the way in the back of the crowd with our baby girl, was shocked to hear her name. She looked up and saw her hubby on the stage holding the mic. (*Some guys buy flowers. I give shoutouts.*) The band eventually finished the song and left the stage, while my other new bandmates and I had our five minutes of fame.

Don't judge me too harshly for not being a good example to my youth group. I apologized to all of them afterward, but oddly enough, after that moment, many of them seemed to appreciate me more and listened more intently when I spoke. I seemed to have earned some kind of street credit with them from this stunt. Aww, the glory days of youth ministry! What sweet memories!

I want you to know, just like there was a scramble for the mic at the Newsboys concert, there is a scramble for the mic in your mind.

Here's what you need to know: Whoever has the mic of your

mind directs your thoughts, and your thoughts will ultimately direct your life.

The two most frequent entities that make their way to the stage to take the mic in your mind are the inner critic of your life and the enemy of your soul.

1) The Inner Critic of Your Life

This is the voice telling you all the time, "You are not pretty enough," "You are not smart enough," "You are not enough." This inner critic of your life is the one who brings all those mean things said to you from the past and plays them back to you on repeat. The truth is we all have this inner critic, and he or she is brutal, harsh, and without any grace.

2) The Enemy of Your Soul

There is a devil, and he is very real. He will most certainly amplify the dark thought bubbles entering your mind. Have you ever been having a really good day, and out of nowhere, a thought enters your mind, and it is a horrible thought? Maybe it is a thought to do something bad. Maybe it's a thought that paralyzes you with fear. I have learned these kinds of thoughts aren't natural. They are supernatural. I have learned to discern these kinds of thoughts as demonic attacks against the mind. This is spiritual warfare against your life. The devil knows once he gets your mind, the heart and body are sure to follow.

Here is the great news for you: As a follower of Jesus, you now have a third option of who gets the mic.

3) The Spirit of God

When the Spirit of God has the mic, your thoughts begin moving in a new direction. This is where the new neural pathways are formed so that your mind can be renewed.

Listen to this Scripture and how the Spirit of God impacts your thoughts:

> Those who live according to the flesh have their minds set on what the flesh desires; but those who live in accordance with the Spirit have their minds set on what the Spirit desires. The mind governed by the flesh is death, but the mind governed by the Spirit is life and peace. (ROMANS 8:5–6 NIV)

Did you catch that?

When your mind is governed by the Spirit of God, there is *life* and *peace*.

As someone who has been possessed by the Spirit of God, you get to choose who governs your mind.

Another way to put it? You get to choose who is on the stage.

Because the Spirit of God now lives in you as a follower of Jesus, God has supernaturally empowered you to be the *stage manager* of your mind. As the *stage manager*, you are the one who gives permission on who gets to take the stage and hold the mic. If you don't like the voice on the mic in your mind, it's time to step in as the *stage manager* and give the mic to the Spirit of God.

I love this Scripture from the Passion translation. The Passion translation is not an authentic translation of Scripture. It's more like a loose paraphrasing of the original Scripture.

> We can demolish every deceptive fantasy that opposes God and break through every arrogant attitude that is raised up in defiance of the true knowledge of God. We capture, like prisoners of war, every thought and insist that it bow in obedience to the Anointed One. (2 CORINTHIANS 10:5 TPT)

This is warfare language.

There's a battle going on in your mind, and you now have the authority to take every thought that is not of God and lock it up.

Fixing Your Thoughts

ONE OF THE Scriptures I love that talks about making a change with our thought life is found in the book of Philippians:

> And now, dear brothers and sisters, one final thing.
> Fix your thoughts on what is true, and honorable,
> and right, and pure, and lovely, and admirable. Think
> about things that are excellent and worthy of praise.
> (PHILIPPIANS 4:8 NLT)

Another translation of this same Scripture uses the word *dwell* in place of the word *fix*. In other words, you choose the thoughts you dwell on.

You may not have control over what thought bubbles jump into your mind throughout the day, but you do have complete control over what thought bubbles you dwell on.

My dad spent his career as an air traffic controller. Before 9/11 and major security upgrades, there was a time when air traffic controllers could bring their kids with them to work. As a little boy, I was able to go up in the tower with my dad and listen to him talk to pilots. He even allowed me to speak to some of the pilots on a few occasions.

Here is what I find so fascinating and why the job is one of the most stressful jobs on the planet: As the air traffic controller, he was the final authority on whether a plane could land. In the same way, you are the air traffic controller of your mind. You are the final authority on whether a thought can land in your mind. Dwelling on a thought gives permission for a thought to land in your mind.

Martin Luther, one of the earliest theologians in the Protestant movement, said this about fixing your thoughts:

> You cannot keep birds from flying over your head, but
> you can keep them from building a nest in your hair.

Still as relevant today as it was centuries ago.

You have the power to fix your thoughts, and this is the key to begin the process of renovating your mind so you can experience a transformed life.

I want to share with you the three big ways to fix your thoughts so you can love God with *all* of your mind.

Fix Your Thoughts on the Word

The Word I am referring to here is Scripture.

The Holy Bible.

The Bible is such a powerful resource for not just our faith, but also for our lives.

Earlier in this section, we talked about loving God with our minds by leveling up with more knowledge of God. The Bible is our main source on doing that. However, we shouldn't be reading the Bible solely for information. We should be reading it for transformation.

In another New Testament Scripture, the apostle Paul, who is writing to the church in Ephesus, makes this beautiful analogy between how husbands ought to love their wives in the same way Jesus loved the church:

> Husbands, love your wives, as Christ loved the church and gave himself up for her, that he might sanctify her, having cleansed her by the washing of water with the word. (EPHESIANS 5:25–26 ESV)

Jesus has prepared the church by washing her with the Word of God.

A few years ago, I borrowed a pressure washer from a friend so I could clean the cement around my house. He didn't just have a regular pressure washer. He had this extra strength one, the kind that required a whole trailer to haul it around. It was so powerful that it required both hands to hold the hose while it was washing. As I went out to begin the pressure washing, I told Tara I would be outside for a couple of hours cleaning up the backyard.

As I started pressure washing the concrete and saw stain after stain disappear, I became obsessed. It was one of the most satisfying jobs I have ever done. I started with the patio, but then I moved to pressure washing all our walkways, then our windows, and went as far as cleaning the whole sidewalk in front of our house. I was having so much fun that I lost track of time. Tara came outside to check on me and told me I had been out there for almost the entire day. Time flies when you're having fun.

I think the most satisfying part of pressure washing was seeing the stains come off and the concrete look so clean.

God has given us a pressure washer for our minds, and it's called the Word of God. It has been given to us to help remove the tough stains that have been caked on our minds for far too long.

Yes, God wants to brainwash you.

The Word is the supercharged pressure washer for your mind for the stains of *stinkin' thinkin'* to be removed.

However, the Word is only going to pressure wash your mind if you're actually opening it, reading it, and listening to what it has to say to you.

I read something really eye-opening a while back. It was a study that was done in 2009 by the Center for Bible Engagement.[15] They issued a report that concluded that people who read the Bible at least four days a week experience exponential transformational benefits. In the study, they polled forty thousand people, ages eight to eighty, and they wanted to see how people were engaging in Scripture. As they compiled the results, they made a profound discovery that they were not even looking for when they originally planned the survey.

The study indicated that when people engaged in the Bible one time a week, which could include hearing a Scripture from a weekend church gathering, there was a negligible effect on some key areas of their lives. The same result was true if people engaged in the Scriptures two times a week. The result equaled little to no effect. Three times a week saw a small change in the behavior of the person engaging in Scripture. The eye opener happened when Bible engagement reached at least four times a week. People who reported reading the Bible four or more times per week experienced an exponential jump in transformation for their lives. The stunning findings included the following:

1. Feelings of loneliness dropped 30 percent.
2. Anger issues dropped 32 percent.

3. Bitterness in relationships dropped 40 percent.
4. Alcoholism dropped 57 percent.
5. Sex outside of marriage dropped 68 percent.
6. Feeling spiritually stagnant dropped 60 percent.
7. Viewing pornography dropped 61 percent.
8. Sharing your faith jumped 200 percent.
9. Discipling others jumped 230 percent.

Not reading the Bible once per week.

Not reading the Bible twice.

Not reading the Bible even three times.

Reading the Bible four or more times a week led to the transformation.

Another study I read recently troubled me greatly. The American Bible Society did a study in 2022 and found that twenty-six million Americans have mostly or completely stopped reading the Bible in the last year.[16]

According to their research, only 39 percent of Americans say they read the Bible multiple times per year or more. This is down by 11 percent from the previous year. It is the steepest and sharpest decline on record.

So, process this with me.

Bible reading in America has declined significantly, while mental health issues have risen sharply.

Is there a connection?

Is there something going on here that maybe we haven't really taken the time to identify?

The Word of God is here to help transform your life, because it's renewing your mind.

Every time you're in the Bible, it's renewing you.

I like to say it this way.

The more you get into the Word of God, the more the Word of God gets into you.

If the devil can't make you bad, he will simply keep you from reading your Bible.

Digestion by Meditation

BEFORE YOU GET superinspired by this and set a goal for yourself, such as reading the whole Bible in a year, I need to give you a word of caution.

The Bible isn't meant to be read like other books, where you read them as quickly as you can so you can finish them. You should read the Bible more like you read the instructions from the IKEA dresser you purchased. When you're reading instructions like this, you have probably stopped after reading a step and read it again to make sure you understand how you are to put things together. That's how you are to read the Bible. The Bible is your instruction manual on how to build a life of abundance that makes a difference in this world.

At the very beginning of the book of Psalms in the Old Testament Scriptures, Psalm 1 begins by giving a glimpse of how to read the Scriptures in a way that will transform your life:

> Blessed is the one who does not walk in step with the
> wicked or stand in the way that sinners take or sit in the
> company of mockers, but whose delight is in the law of
> the LORD, and who meditates on his law day and night.

That person is like a tree planted by streams of water,
which yields its fruit in season and whose leaf does not
wither—whatever they do prospers. (PSALM 1:1–3 NIV)

The law mentioned here is the Word of God. It is the Jewish law
that is part of our Old Testament canon of Scripture.

A person who meditates on the Scriptures is a person who is
flourishing in life.

The word *meditation* can be a little off-putting to some people
because it is associated with a lot of mystical practices in our culture.
This scriptural understanding of meditation is not about going into
some kind of hypnotic trance, but rather it's about reflection and
thought. The best analogy to this understanding of meditating
on God's Word is found in looking at how a cow chews its food.

Most of my childhood was surrounded by livestock animals, so
I have had plenty of experience watching cows chew their food.
Here is a fun fact about cows. They have a very different digestive
system from what we have as humans. They have a four-chambered
stomach, and it requires them to ruminate their food in order to
properly digest it. They'll eat some grass, then put their head up,
chew it for a bit, swallow it, and then burp it up, chewing it some
more, then swallow it again. It's quite a lengthy process. If you
happen to see a cow in a field, it will more than likely be chewing
because of its long digestive process.

Perhaps the better translation for Psalm 1 should be "ruminating"
rather than "meditating." It's through this ruminating that you
properly digest the Word of God and pressure wash your mind.

Through my experience reading the Bible, I have found a very
effective way to ruminate on the Word of God. This is my own
four-chambered digestive system that I have developed to allow my
mind to digest the Word. This way of reading the Scriptures has
really helped me not only level up on my knowledge of God and the

Bible, but it has also helped me understand how God wants to use the words of Scripture to renew my mind and transform my life.

First Digestion—Read It

I know what you are thinking. This is a given. But is it? Chances are that you probably already own a Bible. How often are you actually opening it and reading it? It's not helping you renovate your mind by sitting on your bookshelf. Just because the Bible is in your house doesn't mean it's going to transform your life.

Perhaps a big reason you're not motivated to read the Bible is that you don't own a good Bible. It's probably not very motivating to read great-grandma's King James Version family Bible that weighs close to a thousand pounds. Thee and thy and thou? Who talks like that? I don't mean to diss the King James Version of the Bible. I'm just stating the obvious. It is pretty difficult for most folks to understand.

Owning a great Bible is one of the biggest ways you will be more motivated to open it and read what it has to say to you. Digital versions of the Bible are convenient, but nothing beats an old-school hard copy. There is something so sweet to have actual pages to open, words to underline, notes to write in the margin. Yes, it's OK to write in your Bible. I actually encourage you to.

One of my personal favorite study Bibles is called the Life Application Study Bible. One of the reasons I love this study Bible so much is because of the commentary it features at the bottom of each page. It makes it so much easier to understand the Scriptures. It's like having a group of pastors sitting around you, talking with you about the verses you are reading.

It may cost you in the neighborhood of fifty to eighty dollars to buy one. Before you talk yourself out of spending the money on one, think of how much money a standard college textbook costs you these days. You use it for maybe a semester, and then it collects dust in your garage for the next thirty years. (Yes, I still have a box in my garage of old college textbooks. I'm a hoarder by nature.) We pay the money for these textbooks because we are "investing in our future." Buying a great study Bible is an investment in your eternity.

Besides having a great study Bible, a question I get asked a lot is "What version is the right version to get?" There are quite a few these days:

KJV, NKJV, NAS, ESV, NIV, NLT, GNT, PBS.
(Actually, PBS is not a real version of the Bible. I just wanted to make sure you were paying attention.)

What version should you own? According to most modern-day biblical scholars, the New American Standard Bible, also known as the NASB, is the most accurate translation of the original language (Hebrew, Greek, and Aramaic) from the original manuscripts. Next in line for accuracy in translation would be the English Standard Version, also known as the ESV.

There is a misperception out there that the King James Version is the most accurate translation of the Bible. This is not true. There have been all kinds of new archaeological findings of ancient manuscripts since the King James Version was originally put together. But if you prefer reading words like *thee*, *thy*, and *thou*, this one's for you.

To make the Bible easier to read, some newer translations have been created, such as the New International Version (NIV) and the New Living Translation (NLT). These versions take some liberties in the words they choose for translation, without changing the meaning of the text. For newer followers of Jesus, I like to recommend the New Living Translation. It's a great, easy-to-read version and a good way to start off learning the Word of God in a very understandable way.

Purchasing a good study Bible is a great first step. However, the real transformation takes place in your life when you develop a daily practice of opening it and reading Scripture. Every time you read the Bible, two things happen: First, God's heavenly supercharged pressure washer fires up to remove those old patterns of thinking. Second, the Spirit of God takes the mic of your mind and declares life and peace to you. This great combination is what brings you a renewed mind.

Years ago, our church developed a daily Bible reading plan to encourage everyone to read the Bible every day. The plan includes reading one chapter from the Old Testament and one chapter from the New Testament each day. What is great about a plan like this is that it gets you into a daily habit of opening the Bible and reading it.

Without fail, every time I read those two chapters for the day, God will take at least one verse from those chapters and give me some kind of heavenly thought. His voice begins speaking in the mic of my mind. It could be in the form of conviction over something I did, or it could be encouragement over a direction he wants me to pursue. It could be a confirmation over something I have been hearing through multiple sources.

Here is your challenge if you choose to accept: Take twenty-one days in a row and read your Bible. You are more than welcome to follow our reading plan, or you can find another plan to follow. Just remember, you are reading for the quality, not quantity. Sometimes, less is more when it comes to reading the Bible.

Second Digestion—Write It

I have heard from almost every teacher since the seventh grade that if I take notes from the teacher's lecture, I am more likely to remember the information later. It turns out, my teachers were speaking the truth.

In a study published in the *American Journal of Psychology*, researchers from the University of Notre Dame and Florida State

University found that taking notes facilitated more elaborate mental processing of the material, allowing people to more accurately respond to subsequent memory test questions of the material.[17]

Writing information down helps your mind retain the information better.

When it comes to ruminating on the Word of God, note-taking, or as I refer to it, *journaling*, becomes a great second digestion of the Scriptures you are reading.

Purchasing a small journal to keep with your Bible is a great practice. This is how I have been journaling for years. I have now found the notepad on my smartphone to be an even more effective way to keep my journal entries because I can do a quick Scripture search or even a word search to find a note I have made. So, whether it's in a journal or a digital note on your smartphone, write it down so you can retain it better.

One of the most effective methods I have learned to use in journaling my daily Bible reading is called the *SOAP* method—scripture, observation, application, prayer.

Scripture

I always start my journal entry by writing down the Scripture I am reading at the very top of the page, along with the date. It is superhelpful to have it listed at the top so I can easily find the Scripture reference later.

Observation

Under observation, you simply write down anything that really stands out to you in the chapter you are reading. Ask yourself questions as you read the Scriptures. What's going on? What's this passage about? Who's the author? Who's the author writing to? What's the original purpose of why the author is writing this text in the first place? What's the backstory of the chapter?

Application

This is where the journaling gets fun. Under application, ask yourself some questions:

- How can I apply this Scripture to my personal life?
- How does this speak to me about my marriage?
- How does this speak to me about my relationships or my job or my health or my situation that I'm dealing with internally?

This is where the Spirit of God starts speaking into the mic of your mind. Writing down the answers to these personal questions becomes so valuable because I believe this is where the Spirit of God takes the stage, grabs the mic, and begins to answer your questions. He uses the Scriptures to speak directly into your life.

God's answer for you, God's remedy for you, God's counsel for you, is found in this step of journaling. I call these revelations *heavy revys*, short for "heavenly revelations."

I believe every day God has a *heavy revy* to give me for something I am personally dealing with in my life. These *heavy revys* are waiting for you every time you read the Bible. All it takes is one revelation from heaven to change the trajectory of your entire future. So, make sure to write each one down because you may forget how God spoke to you through the Scriptures.

I can't tell you how many times I have gone back into old journals years after writing them, and God has used those old journal entries from my daily Bible reading to speak to me again. These *heavy revys* are priceless.

Prayer

It's a great practice to end each journal entry with a short personal prayer you can write down in response to the Scripture you read.

Something like this:

> Thank you, Lord, for this beautiful Scripture. I know
> that the Holy Spirit has brought a revelation to me
> through this reading. Help me to live out what you
> have shown me today. In Jesus's name, Amen.

Third Digestion—Share It

Find someone in your circle of life to share your *heavy revys* with.

This is another great way to help you digest the Scriptures even more because in order to explain it to someone else, you really need to have an understanding of it yourself.

Jesus never intended you to live your life with God on your own. Having a squad around you who also love God is critically important. The way I look at it is if Jesus, who was the son of God, found it essential to have close relationships around him, how much more important is it for me to stay close to other followers of Jesus?

I call these special people around me my *battle buddies*.

If you don't have any *battle buddies* for your life, you need to get proactive and go find them. The best place to find some great *battle buddies* for your life is through your local church community. Our church offers a variety of groups that meet during the week to help people find *battle buddies* for their lives.

These *battle buddies* are the ones you can share your *heavy revys* with.

The fun side benefit of sharing your *heavy revys* with these *battle buddies* is that, oftentimes, God will use the revelations he gave to you to encourage your battle buddy in something they are going through. Your *heavy revy* has now also become their *heavy revy*. He doesn't want to just speak to you. He wants to use you to help speak to somebody else.

My wife and I will encourage each other all the time as we share with each other what *heavy revys* God showed us through the daily Bible reading.

The more you share it, the more you'll digest it.

Fourth Digestion—Memorize It

Please don't misunderstand me on this point. I don't memorize every Scripture I read, but I have found it very helpful and transformative to memorize a few verses.

It's not easy for me to do this. Some people are gifted at being able to memorize things easily. I am always so impressed with people who can sing a song by memory without having to look at any lyrics. I can hear a song a hundred times, and I still have to look up the lyrics to sing it correctly.

Even though it is difficult for me to commit things to memory, I forced myself to memorize a dozen different verses from the Bible.

The reason I worked hard at memorizing these verses is that I know the effectiveness it has in overcoming temptation.

Scripture tells us that Jesus had his own battle with temptation.

Isn't it crazy to think Jesus was tempted?

It's recorded in three of the four Gospels. These accounts tell us the devil is the one who was tempting Jesus in the wilderness. The account of the temptation given to us in the Gospel of Matthew reads like the devil is having a full-on conversation with Jesus.

I personally don't feel the devil was visibly standing next to Jesus and audibly speaking to Jesus in this exchange. I believe the devil was more than likely bringing the temptation to Jesus through some thought bubbles. The devil had grabbed hold of the mic in his mind.

Remember: Temptation always begins with a thought.

After every temptation the devil brings Jesus, Jesus returns fire by quoting Scripture back at the devil.

Jesus shows us through his responses that he had committed many of the Hebrew Scriptures to memory, and he used them like bullets in a gun to fire back at the devil.

After the third counterattack, Jesus commands the devil to leave, and he did.

Now, I don't know what things you may be struggling with.

Maybe you struggle with lust.

Maybe you struggle with anger.

Maybe you struggle with body image.

What would you say is a temptation you struggle with?

I believe for every temptation that the devil may launch in your mind, there is a verse from the Bible that can help you overcome it.

One of the first verses I committed to memory was 1 John 4:4:

> You are from God, little children, and have overcome them; because greater is He who is in you than he who is in the world. (1 JOHN 4:4 NASB 1995)

A friend of mine calls this verse "First John 4 by 4." It's a verse that will get you out of the mud of any temptation that is trying to overtake you.

I had this verse written out on a Post-it Note and posted it on the dashboard of my car for years. The biggest issue I had in the early days of following Jesus was not being able to tell myself no. I had zero self-control. I would tell myself, *I'm not going to do that.* And then I would end up giving in.

God gave me such a *heavy revy* in this verse. I felt the Spirit of God tell me, "It's not about you and your ability to resist temptation. It's about me and my power living in you. My power living in you is greater than the power of the enemy coming against you. The more you're leaning into the power that you have in me, the more victory you're going to see over the enemy in your life." Once I learned 1

John 4:4, every time a temptation came my way, I would pray this prayer, "Holy Spirit, give me overcoming strength." Then I would speak the Scripture out loud.

Sometimes I would say it repeatedly.

"Greater is He who is in me than he who is in the world."

It worked. I started experiencing victories over these temptations. God gave me overcoming strength to demonstrate self-control. It wasn't until a few years later that I learned part of the fruit of the Spirit being in my life is self-control.

Praying and quoting Scripture really does work to help us overcome temptation.

Here are a few great verses to consider memorizing to help you be an overcomer in your struggle:

Anxiety

> Cast your cares on the Lord and he will sustain you; he will never let the righteous be shaken.
> (PSALM 55:22 NIV)

Lust

> Blessed are the pure in heart, for they will see God.
> (MATTHEW 5:8 NIV)

Anger

> My dear brothers and sisters, take note of this: Everyone should be quick to listen, slow to speak and slow to become angry. (JAMES 1:19 NIV)

Addiction

> For the Spirit that God has given us does not make us timid; instead, his Spirit fills us with power, love, and self-control. (2 TIMOTHY 1:7 GNT)

Sadness

> The LORD himself goes before you and will be
> with you; he will never leave you nor forsake
> you. Do not be afraid; do not be discouraged.
> (DEUTERONOMY 31:8 NIV)

If I didn't cover a struggle you deal with, take a moment and do a search on your internet browser of choice with the following words:

"a great Bible verse to help me overcome

_____."

Fill in the blank with whatever your struggle is. Your internet search engine will not fail you. There are bound to be a few great Bible verses that pop up on the search for you to choose from.

Think of these memorized verses like bullets in a gun. When the enemy of your soul starts firing these thoughts of temptation at you, you are to return fire at him with these memorized verses. You will overcome the temptation and cause him to flee from you.

Read it.

Write it.

Share it.

Memorize it.

By letting the Scriptures pass through each of these chambers in your mind, your thoughts will be *fixed* on the Word.

I'll leave this section about the Word of God by giving you a quote from Charles Spurgeon that really inspired me to always be meditating on the Word:

> A Bible that's falling apart usually belongs to someone
> who isn't.[18]

Fix Your Thoughts on the Good

BECAUSE WE LIVE in a consumer-driven culture, we are constantly being reminded by TV and social media of what we don't have or what is wrong in our lives.

This can create some negative thought patterns where it's hard to see any good at all in our lives.

The Vulture and the Hummingbird

These two species of birds often frequent the area where I live. What is so fascinating to me is that even though they are in the same environment, they live so differently. The vulture has a diet of decomposing meat from dead animals, and the hummingbird feeds off the nectar of radiant flowers. The vulture will often be spotted circling above a dead animal waiting for the perfect moment to land and begin feasting. The hummingbird, on the other hand, never seems to notice the stench of dead carcasses because it is busy looking for the sweet blossoms of colorful flowers. Each bird finds what it is looking for.

Just like the vulture and the hummingbird, you will more than likely always find what you are looking for. If you look for the bad, you will find the bad. If you look for the good, you will find the good.

Are you actively looking for the good in your life?

According to multiple Scriptures in the Bible, as you love God and run after him, the goodness of God begins running after you.

One of the most popular verses in the whole New Testament that talks about this is found in the book of Romans. It's also found on posters and mugs throughout Hobby Lobby:

And we know that for those who love God all things
work together for good, for those who are called according to his purpose. (ROMANS 8:28 ESV)

The saying we have around our church is, if it's not good, God's
not done. Hang in there. The goodness is going to come.

The greatest way to fix your thoughts on the good is by giving thanks.

I believe this is one of the reasons Scripture tells us it is God's
will for our lives to give thanks:

Give thanks in all circumstances; for this is God's will
for you in Christ Jesus. (1 THESSALONIANS 5:18 NIV)

Giving thanks breaks you out of these negative thought patterns
and elevates the good in your life.

Being *grateful* is an *attitude* you choose. This is why we call it
gratitude.

Gratitude is the key to unlocking a better attitude in you and is
also a big help in renovating your mind.

Thank God for What You Have

When was the last time you made an inventory of all the things
you have? This could range from your spouse to your car to your
kids to your job. You get the point.

Take a moment right now as you are reading this and begin to
think about all you have, and give thanks to God out loud for all
these things.

Giving thanks helps you to see what's there instead of what isn't.

Thank God for What Is Right

We tend to become blind to what is most familiar. As long as something is right in our lives, we stop paying attention to it. In some

cases, we can even take things for granted because we are so familiar with them being right in our lives. I call it becoming *blind to the blessings.*

The practice of giving thanks for what is right in our lives not only helps reorient our thought patterns and keep us from becoming blessing blind but also allows us to appreciate things a lot more.

Take a moment and thank God for the things that are right in your life. Thank God for your health. Thank God for your family being together. Thank God for making a relationship with him possible.

Thank God for What Didn't Happen

Let's be honest. There are lots of things that could be so much worse in your life. If God had not intervened in a moment of your life, your life could look so different from what it does right now.

As I look back on my poor choices as an adolescent and even into my young adult years, I am so grateful for all that didn't happen to me. I am convinced that if I had not fully surrendered to God when I did, I would not be alive today.

Take a moment and thank God right now for all that didn't happen in your life.

As you immerse yourself in all this thanksgiving, it not only renews your mind but also fills you with peace.

With anxiety being such a big issue these days for so many people, I think it's worth noting one of the remedies Scripture gives us to help us overcome anxiety in our lives is giving thanks:

> Do not be anxious about anything, but in every situation, by prayer and petition, with thanksgiving, present your requests to God. And the peace of God, which transcends all understanding, will guard your hearts and your minds in Christ Jesus. (PHILIPPIANS 4:6–7 NIV)

Did you catch that part about "thanksgiving"?

Thanksgiving is part of God's prescription for you to empty yourself of anxiety and experience his peace in your mind.

Once more, it's fun to point out that recent scientific research has confirmed what the Bible has been telling us for thousands of years.

Dr. Paul Mills, a professor of family medicine and public health at the University of California, San Diego School of Medicine, did a study on the health benefits of being grateful. He recruited 186 men and women, average age sixty-six, who already had some damage to their hearts, either through years of sustained high blood pressure or as a result of a heart attack or even an infection of the heart itself. They each filled out a standard questionnaire to rate how grateful they felt for the people, places, or things in their lives.

It turned out that the more grateful people were, the healthier they were. "They had less depressed mood, slept better, and had more energy."[19]

Researchers at the University of Manchester in England looked at how gratitude might affect people's sleep. Their study included over four hundred adults of all ages—40 percent with sleep disorders—who completed questionnaires that asked about gratitude, sleep, and presleep thoughts. Gratitude was related to having more positive thoughts and fewer negative ones at bedtime. This, in turn, was associated with dozing off faster and sleeping longer and better.[20]

As you give thanks, you fix your thoughts on the good and, as a result, your mind gets renewed.

Fix Your Thoughts on the Pure

TARA AND I live in a neighborhood surrounded by some open land, inhabited by all kinds of wildlife. We have frequent visitors in our backyard, including squirrels, lizards, and sometimes snakes. I love to sit in our backyard and soak in the beauty of God's creation. With the weather so nice most of the time, I unfortunately got in the habit of leaving the door open while I was outside. I honestly didn't think anything about doing this until, one day, I was in our bedroom. I went to grab something off my nightstand, and while I was doing this, something else fell off and landed behind it. As I looked behind the nightstand and lowered myself to grab the item that had fallen, I happened to see these two little eyes staring at me from under my bed. It was a lizard looking right at me.

Now, I'm not scared of lizards, but someone who lives with me is terrified of them, and she happens to sleep in the same bed with me, where this lizard was currently underneath. I thought about this for a moment. If I told my wife there was a lizard loose in our bedroom, she would never come into the bedroom again. It would be over. We were going to have to move. So I was looking straight at this lizard. He knew I saw him, and he was still like a statue. I prayed a quick prayer, "Help me, Jesus." I walked over to the door in our bedroom and quietly and carefully opened it. I then got down under the bed and put my hand behind him to encourage him to walk out the door. He moved out from behind the bed quickly, and I started to get concerned he wasn't going out the door but into our closet instead. At this point, I was talking to the little serpent. "Don't go in there, little guy. Go outside. I want to sleep with my wife again. Pretty please." I nudged him a little bit. He moved a little bit out, and then he went out the door and back out into the wilderness. Thank you, Jesus!

Right after this, I went into the living room, and I was able to tell Tara what had happened because the lizard was gone. Ever since that moment, I have been supercareful to close the doors because I found out critters like to come in and hang out under our bed when I leave the doors open.

In the same way, your mind is like a house. It has doors and walls to it as well. If you aren't careful and leave some doors open, don't be surprised to find some critters taking up residence in your mind, making it extremely difficult for you to love God with *all* your mind.

I have seen an evolution in church culture over the last few decades. There has been this very subtle and slow change in many church people's moral standards when it comes to the entertainment they consume.

I can remember a time in the early '90s when I first fully surrendered my life to Jesus, when no real Christian would dare watch an R-rated movie or listen to anything but Christian music.

As I look back, there was, for sure, a very legalistic mentality in the church, but I believe it was coming from a place of trying to protect our minds from unhealthy and unhelpful thought bubbles. When you are watching naked bodies on the screen or hearing provocative lyrics in a song, it's hard to argue that those things aren't having an influence on your thought life.

Input Determines Output

E NTERTAINMENT.

Have you ever thought about the word *entertainment?* E-N-T-E-R are the first letters of this word.

The shows you're watching, the music you're listening to, and the social media accounts you are following are all "entering" your mind.

To really love God with *all* your mind, you must close the doors and seal up any holes in the wall.

In the Hebrew Scriptures, there is a book called Nehemiah that gives an account of how the city of Jerusalem was rebuilt after the Israelites had been taken into exile. Nehemiah is given the duty of overseeing the rebuilding of the city. His first observation when he rode around the city to assess the damages was the horrific shape the city was in because the walls were knocked down and the gates were burned. In order to be a thriving city again, the walls had to be rebuilt and the gates had to be restored. It was the only way the people living in the city could be protected from the invaders who were having their way with the unprotected people in Jerusalem. Nehemiah, in fact, rebuilt the walls and restored the gates, and the city was resurrected.

In order to love God with *all* of your mind, you are going to have to rebuild some walls and restore some gates in your mind. The benefit for you will be less struggle with some of those unhealthy and unhelpful thought bubbles brought in by poor entertainment choices.

Throughout my entire adult life, I have felt a little out of the loop sometimes being around some people discussing a new series they have binged on Netflix, an artist's new album that dropped, or a celebrity's latest Instagram story. But for my own mind's sake, I am OK feeling a little out of the loop around people so I can have less of a struggle with my thought life.

There is a saying I have heard all my life:

"Garbage in, garbage out."

The call of God is to love him with *all* of your mind. To do this effectively, you will have to close some doors to prevent the critters from getting in.

What is really unsettling for me as a pastor and church leader is seeing a significant rise in our young adult population using mind-altering drugs, such as marijuana, mushrooms, and other hallucinogens. They're making a comeback.

Drugs like these are a major way for critters to get into your mind. I'm not talking about tiny lizards. I am talking Komodo-dragon-sized lizards.

In most of the deliverances I have been a part of, some kind of drug use was part of the person's past.

In my former days of being a part-time Christian, I remember one day looking in the mirror, getting ready to go somewhere after I had just taken some serious hits on a bong. As I was looking in the mirror, my face distorted, and I saw the most hideous monster looking at me through the mirror. Was I tripping? One hundred percent. But I sobered up quickly after that moment, and I realized I was subjecting not only my mind to demonic entities, but I was also opening up my whole entire life to them. I have no doubt I had demonic spirits manipulating me while I was using drugs.

Take it from me. Get rid of the drugs and close the door. They are not helping you. They are harming you.

The second part of *fixing* your mind on what is pure is being intentional to choose some new inputs for your mind.

- This is where music that lifts up the name of Jesus comes in.
- This is where wholesome family movies without nudity or violence comes in.
- This is where choosing to follow only social media accounts that inspire your faith comes in.

The entertainment you choose to plug into makes a big difference in the thoughts that you think.

Yes, you may come off looking like a prude to people around you who may not understand the reason why you don't watch certain shows, why you only listen to music that sings about Jesus, or why you only follow a limited number of people on social media.

But what's more important: how people view you or your ability to think about what is pure so you can love God with *all* of your mind?

Let's be a people who love God not just with some of our mind but with *all* of our mind.

If you want to experience the awe of God, you have to start living in the *all* of God, and that most definitely includes your mind.

DISCUSSION QUESTIONS FOR PART 2

All My Mind

- How can we intentionally increase our knowledge of God and his Word in a way that deepens our love for him, rather than just accumulating facts?

- This section talks about the war in our minds and the importance of "preparing" our thoughts. What practical steps can we take to *fight* this war daily?

- The concept of neuroplasticity shows that our brains can change. How does this scientific truth reinforce the biblical call to be transformed by the renewing of our minds?

- What are some common thought patterns or *thought bubbles* that you find yourself battling daily? How do these thoughts influence your relationship with God?

- What are some *stinkin' thinkin'*, or negative thought patterns, you struggle with, and how can Scripture help you replace those thoughts with truth?

- How can we practically "demo" or eliminate old, destructive thought patterns to make room for new, godly thinking?

- As you think of your neural pathways as well-trodden trails, how might you cultivate new, healthier thought patterns that align with God's Word? What habits or practices can help reinforce these new pathways?

- What are some specific Scriptures you can memorize or meditate on to combat *stinkin' thinkin'* and promote positive, godly thoughts? How will you incorporate these into your daily routine?

- When it comes to reading the Bible, what do you find is the most challenging part that discourages you from reading it on a regular basis? What steps could you take to help motivate yourself to read it daily?

- This section emphasizes loving God with all your mind, including your thoughts. What is one specific action you can take this week to better align your thoughts with God and his Word?

PART 3

ALL MY HEART

The battle line between good and evil runs through the heart of every man.

—ALEKSANDR SOLZHENITSYN

AS WE CONTINUE our journey in learning what it means to love God with our *all*, we are now going to move from the head down to the heart.

It seems as though Scripture talks about the heart more than all the other cylinders in this *greatest of all time* commandment.

The heart is mentioned almost a thousand times in the Bible.

In most cases, when Scripture talks about the heart, it's not referring to the vital organ in your body that is circulating your blood and keeping you alive.

The Greek word for *heart* in this *GOAT* commandment we have been looking at from the Gospel of Mark is the word *kardia*. One of the ways this word is described by the outline of biblical usage from the Blue Letter Bible App is "the seat of the sensibilities, affections, emotions, desires, appetites, and passions."[21]

In short, the heart is the emotional center of your life.

It's the part of you that compels you, motivates you, fuels you, and moves you.

It's the part of you that makes you feel sad, glad, or mad.

It's the part of you that gives you the "feels."

We all have these "feels" to some degree. The spectrum is wide, from some people who are deep feelers and feel everyone's emotions around them to others who are very stoic and hardly ever show emotions to anyone.

I don't think we talk about our feelings and emotions very much because, for whatever reason, it seems they have a negative stigma attached to them, like it's a bad thing to get emotional.

Have you ever had someone say to you, "Quit being so emotional"?

Emotions are a good thing. Without them, we would all be like the Tin Man in *The Wizard of Oz*.

I believe emotions are not just a good thing. I believe they are a God thing. After all, he's the one who created us with them. Here is a crazy, fun fact. Scripture tells us God has a heart:

> After removing Saul, he made David their king. God testified concerning him: "I have found David son of Jesse, a man after My own heart; he will do everything I want him to do." (ACTS 13:22 NIV)

Have you ever just paused and considered the significance of that statement?

God has a heart.

Throughout Scripture, we read about God being glad. We also read about him being sad. We even read about him getting mad.

Yes, God is emotional.

As humans, we are separated from all other species because we have been created in the image of God. In Latin, it is referred to as the "Imago Dei." I love this about us. We are the walking billboards of the "imago dei" and our emotions are proof of that.

Confessions of a Pastor

I cried watching the recent *Little Mermaid* movie. I'm kind of embarrassed to admit that. As Ariel the mermaid was in the middle of one of her songs, my eyes just started pumping out tears. I was overwhelmed with emotions, partly because I was feeling very sentimental watching the movie in the theater with my two adult daughters and my wife. I just kept thinking of my girls being all grown up now. As I realized I was in a full-blown cryfest, I started quickly wiping the tears away. But then I started thinking, *Well, maybe everyone is crying.* I looked over at my daughters. They weren't crying at all, not even a tear. At this point, I was really embarrassed. My wife looked over at me and said, "Are you crying?" I quickly responded, "No. It's allergies," and then quickly turned away. My girls got a great laugh out of that moment. Me? I just cried some more.

What is it for you? What gets you emotional?

Maybe it's not *The Little Mermaid*, but instead, it's watching your favorite sports team. I know many of my friends who have danced in front of their TV sets as their team won the big game. I know others who have actually broken their TV sets because their team lost the big game.

Maybe for you, it's a relationship with another person that has made you emotional. Things started getting tough, an argument broke out, and a breakup ensued, leaving you full of sadness and a bunch of tears.

The bottom line is it's normal to have feelings and show emotions. This demonstrates that you actually have a heart and you're not a robot.

What makes the heart so important, and why I believe the Bible talks so much about it, is the influence it has on how you live.

The emotions inside you become the fuel to launch you. They work like a starter works in your vehicle. It gets the engine running to ultimately get you moving.

Your affections are deep currents that steer your life. Think of them like the rudder of a ship. The rudder literally directs where the ship goes.

Your affections influence your actions and your desires determine your destiny.

This is why the call of God on your life is to love him with *all* of your heart. It ensures you will be driven to God's destiny and purpose for your life.

If you are loving God with only some of your heart, it leaves room for other affections and desires in your heart that have the potential to reroute you to an entirely different destination.

In the Hebrew Scriptures, there was a prophet named Jeremiah who gave a very serious warning about how vulnerable the heart is:

> The heart is more deceitful than all else and is desperately sick; Who can understand it? (JEREMIAH 17:9 NAS)

The one part of you that is the easiest to manipulate, exploit, and deceive is your heart, the epicenter of your emotional self.

This is why I tell people all the time when I am counseling them, "Your feelings are real, but it doesn't mean they're necessarily right."

Have you ever had someone tell you something about another person that made you supermad? Perhaps you got so mad that you actually confronted the person. Then, after explaining to them what you heard from another person, they responded by telling you none of what you heard was true? I can't tell you how many times this has happened to me. I have had feelings flood my system, only to discover later on that none of those things I heard were even true.

Such a waste of emotional energy. It doesn't take much to fire up the heart, and if it is not fully under the control of the love of God, your life can be driven into a brick wall quickly.

Another important warning we have in Scripture that highlights the vulnerability of the heart is found in the book of Proverbs:

> Guard your heart above all else, for it determines the course of your life. (PROVERBS 4:23 NLT)

The NIV translation uses the words *wellspring of life.*

This is a fountain, an artesian spring, which bubbles up and is the source of everything else.

The wellspring of life, the very essence of what makes you alive, is found in these affections, feelings, and desires from your heart.

Because your heart determines the course of your life, the author of this Proverb (more than likely Solomon, the wisest person to ever live, according to the Bible) says your heart needs a TSA security checkpoint. This way, your vulnerable heart will be protected against any harmful affections or desires trying to sneak in and steer you in the wrong direction for your life.

The wisest way to live your life is to have security measures in place to keep unhealthy emotions, affections, and desires out of your heart.

According to the National Center for Health Statistics, heart disease is the leading cause of death among Americans.[22] So many people die every day from a bad heart.

A bad emotional heart can also kill you. It can kill you from experiencing the awe of God in your life. It can kill you from experiencing God's plans and purposes for your life.

The Hebrew Scriptures give us a well-documented history of the monarchy of the ancient kingdoms of Israel and Judah. Every time I read through these Scriptures about the kings of old, it always catches my attention how the kings whose hearts were *fully* devoted to God experienced blessings, reigned as kings for long periods of time, and the kingdom thrived under their leadership, compared to the kings who were not *wholeheartedly* devoted to God. The kings who were not *wholeheartedly* devoted to God seemed to experience so much struggle, often reigning for very short periods of time and having their kingdom suffer under their leadership.

A great example of this can be found in 1 Kings 15.

A Tale of Two Kings

In the eighteenth year of the reign of Jeroboam son of Nebat, Abijah became king of Judah, and he reigned in Jerusalem three years. His mother's name was Maakah, daughter of Abishalom. He committed all the sins his father had done before him; his heart was not fully devoted to the Lord his God, as the heart of David his forefather had been. (1 KINGS 15:1–3 NIV)

DID YOU CATCH that?

King Abijah only reigned for three years. Why?

His heart was not *fully* devoted to God.

The very next king of Judah was King Asa. In this same chapter, we learn that Asa reigned a whopping forty-one years.

What was the difference?

Although he did not remove the high places, Asa's heart was fully committed to the Lord all his life.
(1 KINGS 15:14 NIV)

These two kings are great examples for us on just how important the heart is and what a vital role it plays in where we end up in our lives.

This is why I am convinced the best way to guard your heart is to gorge your heart with as much God as possible.

When your heart is full of God, it forces your heart to light up the no vacancy sign for any unhealthy affections or desires that may want to take up residence in your heart and try to steer you away from the destination God has for your life.

Guard your heart above all else.

Check Your Heart Monitor

NOW THAT WE'VE identified what your heart is and why you need to be careful with it and protect it, it's time to take a look at what is actually already inside it.

Did you know God installed a heart monitor in our bodies? It's called the mouth.

Listen to these words of Jesus:

> For what has been stored up in your hearts will be
> heard in the overflow of your words! (MATTHEW 12:34 TPT)

You can't see a person's heart, but you can get a peek of what's inside their heart by watching their words.

The heart controls what you want, what you do, and ultimately what you say.

Pay attention to your words. They will show you the condition of your heart.

Here's a great way to check the condition of your heart. I call this one the hammer test. Grab a hammer and a nail. Then go drive the nail into a board somewhere. As the hammer misses the nail and hits your thumb instead, pay attention to the words that come out of your mouth.

Trust me! I have done it several times, by accident, of course. The hammer test is very revealing. I am proud to say that, somewhere around fifteen years ago, the words leaving my mouth after slamming my thumb with the hammer had an extreme makeover. A lot fewer curse words and a lot more *hallelujahs*.

I don't really encourage you to do the hammer test. I just think it's a fun way to get you thinking about how much the words you say reveal what is in your heart.

Have you ever been talking to someone and, right in the middle of a sentence, you caught yourself saying something you never intended to say? The words just kind of slipped out of your mouth?

According to Jesus, words don't just slip out of the mouth. They bubble up directly from the heart. Your words are revealing what's already inside you, what's been brewing and festering in your heart.

Your words not only reveal what's in your heart but also what has hold of your heart.

This explains why when you have deep affections and passions about something or someone, you share it with others.

As you think of all the conversations this past week that you have had with other people, what was the recurring subject of your conversations? What did you talk most often about?

Maybe it was politics?

Maybe it was money?

Maybe it was golf?

Maybe it was family?

I want you to know that whatever you spend the most time talking about reveals a lot about what's in your heart.

Whatever has captured your heart also has captured your mouth.

When you are loving God with *all* of your heart, the words flowing from your mouth will involve God and your relationship with him.

How often has God come up in your conversation with others this past week?

How often did you talk about your faith with others this past week?

Do you recall bringing up the name of Jesus in any of your conversations this past week?

I am not asking these questions to make you feel bad or shame you. I want to simply make you aware of your heart condition.

According to Jesus, what is in your heart will be revealed by your words.

When your heart is *full* of Jesus, you will naturally talk about him in some way or another in the conversations you have with other people.

One of the chief Scriptures used to help people solidify their relationship with God and know they are saved is this passage found in the book of Romans:

> If you confess with your mouth Jesus as Lord and believe in your heart that God raised him from the dead, you will be saved. (ROMANS 10:9 NIV).

The proof of what we believe in our hearts comes from what we say with our words.

If someone's heart is *full* of Jesus, you will know it in a ten-minute conversation with them. Jesus will be talked about. Faith will be talked about. The Bible will be talked about. It will bubble up in some way in the conversation.

Confessing Jesus as Lord isn't just about securing your salvation, even though it is definitely a part of it. This Scripture is speaking directly about your heart condition. The words flowing from your mouth become the evidence that Jesus is supremely in charge of your life.

The words you use are a great way for you to be able to see what's in your heart, but there is also one more way to check your heart.

Heavenly Emotional Intelligence

L **ATELY, I HAVE** been saturated with podcasts from different podcasters sharing on the subject of *emotional intelligence*. It's a hot topic these days. In case you haven't heard of this, let me try to give you a quick run-down of what it is. Your *emotional intelligence*, sometimes called your EQ, refers to your ability to recognize, understand, and manage your emotions, as well as perceive and help influence the emotions of others. I am sure you can think of a few people in your life who you would rate as having low EQs. Let me just say I think there is room for improvement for all of us when it comes to our EQ numbers.

Recognizing your emotions is a fundamental part of your EQ. It's often considered the first step in *emotional intelligence* because you need to be aware of how you're feeling before you can manage or respond to those emotions effectively.

Recognizing your emotions when it comes to your relationship with God is vitally important to understanding the condition of your heart.

When your heart is *full* of Jesus, you will have your own internal emotional gauge helping you recognize that your affections, desires, and passions belong to him. Sometimes it's going to manifest through crying while attending a church gathering. The music is flowing, and so are your tears. Sometimes it's going to manifest through excitement. The pastor is speaking, and you get hit with these goosebumps where every hair on your arm stands at attention. I really believe, in moments like these, the presence of God is touching your heart and your body is simply responding to that touch of heaven on your life. This experience of getting emotional toward God or anything having to do with your pursuit of God is normal.

I'm not saying your relationship with God is exclusively about feelings, but feelings are definitely part of the package. They are in any relationship you have. Why would your relationship with God be any different? When you love God with *all* your heart, you are going to *feel* it.

Before you dismiss this and label yourself as a person who doesn't get emotional in your relationship with God, I want to revisit something I mentioned earlier. Is there any time where you have shown emotions in the past?

That sports game?

That friend telling you how much you mean to them?

That party where everyone was dancing and you started throwing your hands up in the air like you just don't care?

There are rare occasions when some people have a condition called alexithymia.[23] Those who have been diagnosed with this condition report never having any kind of emotions in any situation. I want to highlight that this condition is not common.

If you can recall showing emotions in other places for other reasons in the past, what makes you think you shouldn't feel anything when it comes to your relationship with God?

Years ago, I was on the treadmill at the gym. Typically, I have headphones on, and I'm listening to a podcast while I'm working out. As I went to select the podcast for the day, I had this desire come over me to listen to worship music instead of a podcast. So I went to my favorite worship music playlist, pressed play, jumped on the treadmill, and started my workout. About six minutes into the workout, my heart was getting so flooded by my gratitude when thinking of all God was doing in me and for me. I was in the middle of a crowded gym, and at that moment, I felt like it was just me and God in the room alone. The tears started flowing, and without even thinking about it, my hands went straight up. I was in full praise mode in the middle of the gym. My heart was *full* of God, and my body naturally followed.

I am not telling you this story to try to convince you I love Jesus more than you do. I know I am wired more on the spectrum of being hyperemotional. (Remember: I cried watching *The Little Mermaid*.) I simply want to point out to you that when you are close to God, you are going to *feel* it with your heart. Why wouldn't you want to express those feelings to God?

If you can give a shout to the television screen when your favorite team wins the game, certainly you can give a shout of praise to the God that saved your life. There should be some feelings of excitement in you, bubbling up from that emotional center of your being. Don't let anyone convince you that your relationship with God has nothing to do with your feelings. If you are loving God with *all* your heart, you are definitely going to *feel* it.

There is a beautiful story in the Gospels involving a woman who interrupted a dinner party where Jesus and his friends were eating:

> When one of the Pharisees invited Jesus to have dinner with him, he went to the Pharisee's house and reclined at the table. A woman in that town who lived a sinful life learned that Jesus was eating at the Pharisee's house, so she came there with an alabaster jar of perfume. As she stood behind him at his feet, weeping, she began to wet his feet with her tears. Then she wiped them with her hair, kissed them, and poured perfume on them. (LUKE 7:36–38 NIV)

Jesus didn't correct her behavior. He actually rewarded her behavior by telling her she was forgiven.

Not only is it permissible to show your affections to God, but also, I would say, when you love God with *all* your heart, it is to be expected.

Speaking of the ancient kings of Israel and Judah, remember the one who was the man after God's own heart?

King David was so overwhelmed with emotions at the sacred ark of the covenant returning to Jerusalem that Scripture tells us he stripped off his outer clothing and danced like no one was watching.

> Wearing a linen ephod, David was dancing before the Lord with all his might, while he and all Israel were bringing up the ark of the Lord with shouts and the sound of trumpets. As the ark of the Lord was entering the City of David, Michal daughter of Saul watched from a window. And when she saw King David leaping and dancing before the Lord, she despised him in her heart. (2 SAMUEL 6:14–16 NIV).

> When David returned home to bless his household, Michal daughter of Saul came out to meet him and said, "How the king of Israel has distinguished himself today, going around half-naked in full view of the slave girls of his servants as any vulgar fellow would!" David said to Michal, "It was before the Lord, who chose me rather than your father or anyone from his house when he appointed me ruler over the Lord's people Israel—I will celebrate before the Lord. I will become even more undignified than this." (2 SAMUEL 6:20–22 NIV).

When your heart is *full* of love for God, expect your body to respond.

Let the tears flow.

Let the hands raise.

And as David beautifully demonstrated, let the dancing begin.

Heart Blockage That Leads to Heart Stoppage

I'M NO CARDIOLOGIST, but I know enough about the heart in my body that if there is any blockage taking place in the arteries pumping blood into my heart, it's going to lead to some catastrophic results for me.

The same is true for the *kardia*—that emotional center of your life.

Sometimes a blockage can take place in this emotional center, and it can have catastrophic results for us emotionally, spiritually, mentally, and even sometimes physically.

In my experience as a pastor, I have prayed and counseled with countless people who struggle with matters of the heart. People who want to do right and live godly lives, but something in their hearts just seems to be stuck, blocking them from experiencing full-throttle passion for God.

There can be so many reasons why a person struggles in this area of loving God with *all* of their heart, but if I had to choose the two biggest reasons, I would say it is what I call *Gospel blindness* and *strongholds of the heart*.

Gospel Blindness

FIRST, LET ME explain what I mean by *Gospel blindness.*
We become blind to what we're familiar with. If something
is in front of us all the time, we stop paying attention to it.

Let me give you an example.

You walk into your house after being gone on a two-week vacation. As you open the door, an odor meets your nose that almost
knocks you off your feet because it's so bad. Someone left a dirty, wet
rag out before you left for your vacation, and now the whole house
stinks. You get distracted by bringing all the luggage in and forget
about the rag. Two hours go by, and you are no longer noticing the
stench of the dirty rag. Then a friend comes over to your house.
As soon as they walk in the door, they also almost fall over and
say, "What is that horrible smell?" The rag didn't magically stop
smelling. Your nose got used to it, making you what is commonly
referred to as being "nose blind."

For many people who have been followers of Jesus for some time,
they unfortunately become what I call *Gospel blind.*

What I mean by that term is that it is possible to be inoculated
with the message of the cross so much that eventually you stop
seeing the value of it.

Without seeing value in the Gospel, you will have a very difficult
time loving God with your heart.

Jesus himself told us this in the most famous sermon he ever
preached:

> For where your treasure is, there your heart will also
> be. (MATTHEW 6:21 NIV)

Read this again slowly. "Where your treasure is... your heart will also be."

Treasure is something that has extreme value.

Jesus is clearly saying the devotion of your heart is determined by whatever you value as your greatest treasure.

Your affections, desires, and passions are the outcome of what you treasure.

Maybe the problem isn't necessarily that you're not an emotional person when it comes to your faith in Jesus. Maybe the problem is you've stopped noticing the incredible value Jesus has for your life and for your family.

Years ago, when my son Josiah was only eleven years old, I asked him if he would be willing to allow me to use him as a sermon prop for our Easter Sunday message. I've used many sermon props before, but never my one and only son. He asked a few questions and then said, "I'm in." I drove him to the store so he and I could buy matching shirts to wear that Sunday.

In the middle of my Easter message, I began speaking about the incredible value the cross has for all of our lives. One of my friends had built this great-looking cross that I had standing in the middle of the stage for that Easter message. As I was sharing about this, I had Josiah join me on stage. Then, I asked him to put himself on the cross. With little straps, my friend installed on that cross, Josiah strapped himself in and stood there. The feelings I had in that moment were overwhelming. Even though we had rehearsed this together, when it actually happened in the middle of my message, I could barely speak. The whole auditorium was silent as they saw my one and only son attached to this cross. Everyone that day understood a little more deeply the significance and the value of the cross for their lives.

The reason I did this on that Easter Sunday, and the reason I'm bringing this up to you in this book, is because I think sometimes we hear stories in the Bible and disassociate the stories from our own realities.

As Josiah was on the cross, I started explaining to the Easter gathering, if someone really close to me, who loves me, found themselves in a really bad, life-and-death hostage situation, and I found out the only way they can be saved from dying was my son trading places with them, I have to be honest: I don't know if I could let that happen. I don't think I'd be able to sacrifice my own son, even for somebody who really authentically loves me. I don't know if I could make that decision.

As Josiah hung on the makeshift cross, I continued with another scenario.

Suppose this same hostage trade involved a person who wasn't close to me. Matter of fact, let's say this person in the past had actually insulted me. They had said terrible things about me. There is no way in the world I would let my son be traded for them.

As I was telling the whole gathering this scenario, I looked at my little son, and I just began weeping. I began weeping because I was overwhelmed with the incredible value of what God has done for my life.

Jesus really died on a cross to take my place. He did this, not because I deserved it or because I was even close to him.

Scripture actually tells us he did this for us while we were still enemies to God.

> You see, at just the right time, when we were still powerless, Christ died for the ungodly. Very rarely will anyone die for a righteous person, though for a good person someone might possibly dare to die. But God demonstrates his own love for us in this: While we were still sinners, Christ died for us. (ROMANS 5:6–8 NIV)

Let that simmer in your heart for a minute.

More than likely, I wouldn't give my son's life for even someone that was near and dear to my heart, but I certainly wouldn't sacrifice him for my enemy.

But God did.

Jesus took our place so you and I could be set free and experience the life God always intended us to have, where we thrive as citizens of the kingdom of heaven, where God reigns as king of our lives.

As you embrace this incredible value of the cross and begin treasuring what God has done for your life, it's going to impact your heart:

> "For where your treasure is, there your heart will
> be also."

Listen to this Scripture where Jesus describes just how valuable the kingdom of heaven is:

> The kingdom of heaven is like *treasure* hidden in a
> field. When a man found it, he hid it again, and then
> in his *joy*, went and sold *all* he had and bought that
> field. (emphasis added) (MATTHEW 13:44 NIV)

Jesus wants you and me to know the incredible value the kingdom of heaven has for our lives.

It's like this man who finds this treasure and sells everything he owns and gives up everything he has so that he can buy the field and own the treasure it contains.

That's what the kingdom of heaven is like.

It's priceless.

Let's make this super personal.

Imagine your bank called you today and told you the mortgage on your house was paid in full. As you inquire about the person who had paid it off, they tell you a name you have never heard before. Let's say the name is Joe California. You get Joe's phone number and call him to ask why. He tells you he's a billionaire, and once a year, he chooses a name from the bank's mortgage list to bless them by paying off their mortgage. He tells you your name was the one that was chosen this year. If you are a normal person, you would be beyond emotional at this point. What an incredible gift. You would forever be grateful to Joe California.

I want you to know something even better than paying off your mortgage has taken place for you. Another man, Jesus Christ, gave his life for you, to pay off your debt and give you the keys not to a house, but the keys to the kingdom of heaven. It's yours.

The kingdom of heaven is not just a place you go when you die. It's a kingdom that activates in you while you are alive.

Jesus died to get you into heaven, but he resurrected to get heaven into you.

This news ought to fill you with inexpressible joy and gratitude.

When you truly understand the extreme value of what Jesus has made available for your life, loving him with *all* your heart will be your natural response.

The best way to say it is this:

In order for the heart to love Jesus *completely*, it has to treasure him *supremely*.

Why? Because our affections are the outcome of what we treasure.

If you want to be more passionate in your relationship with God and break through this blockage of being *Gospel blind*, then I encourage you to think long and hard about the incredible value of this unshakable kingdom you are now a part of.

The best way to rediscover this treasure living in you is through worship.

Worship is the act of showing value to something or someone.

I heard something years ago from one of my mentors, and it stuck with me. Worship can be defined as "worth-ship."

When you worship, you're ascribing *worth* to someone or something out of a response to what they mean for your life.

When I worship God, I am appreciating his *worth* for my life. The more I value God, the more my heart is going to be *full* of love toward him. The more my heart is *full* of love toward him, the more I want to ascribe *worth* toward him. I call this a holy snowball effect, producing a heart that *fully* and *completely* loves God.

If you want to love God with *all* your heart, you must treasure him supremely. If you want to treasure him supremely, you must worship.

Let me cover what I feel are the three biggest ways to worship God.

Worship Through Singing

MUSIC SEEMS TO have a special connection with our hearts. Have you ever experienced some emotions when you have been listening to a song?

A good *love* song can really hit your heart hard.

And there have been so many throughout the ages.

Here is a fun fact for you: According to *Billboard* magazine, "Endless Love" by Diana Ross and Lionel Richie is the *GOAT* (*greatest of all time*) love song. It topped the *Billboard* charts for nine weeks in a row in 1981.[24]

Long live the '80s!

One of my favorite radio personalities is a woman named Delilah. (Some of you who are familiar with her show are singing her name right now in your head.) She hosts a nationally syndicated radio show where listeners call in and dedicate songs to people they love. I love to hear Delilah talk with a caller who tells her this epic love story, and then she plays a love song that perfectly ties in with that story.

The best way to understand the incredible power of worship through singing is by thinking of this kind of worship as your opportunity to dedicate a love song to God for the gratitude you have for him.

When it comes to your relationship with God and loving him with *all* your heart, I believe music can be one of the most effective ways to see the great worth God has for your life.

There is something so life-giving about worship through music.

You are literally appreciating the value of God for your life when you are singing songs that are thanking him for what he has done, what he is doing, and what he has promised he is going to do for you.

David, who wrote half of the Psalms found in our Bibles, had a definite affinity toward ascribing worth to God through music. This is the same man who was given the title "a man after God's own heart." He wrote song after song about his love for God and just how grateful he was for all God had done for him and his nation.

David was a worshipper, and because of that, he seemed to never become blind to the incredible value of having God in his life.

Singing becomes a way of reminding your heart of just how much God means to you.

I don't understand how some people can be moved to shout and cheer for their favorite sports team, but not be moved to shout and cheer for God:

- Who gave up his one and only Son for them to be forgiven
- Who has prepared a place for them in heaven
- Who has given them his Spirit to live in their bodies to be overcomers
- Who has given them authority over demonic principalities
- Who has blessed them with more than they could ask or imagine

I want to start singing and shouting just writing these things out.

If you want to break through the blockage, take a few minutes and worship God through some songs.

One of the many benefits of technology and digital music is the easy availability you have to an endless number of songs to worship to. My personal favorite is Spotify. It is a digital music app where you pay a monthly subscription fee and get unlimited access to all kinds of music, including worship music. You can also create custom playlists of your favorite songs or follow other people's created playlists. If you want to follow my favorite worship music playlist on Spotify, look me up. My handle is pjcrews777.

Sometimes, the most life-giving exercise for my heart is to throw some AirPods in and listen to twenty minutes of anointed worship music.

Worship Through Giving

IT WAS NINETEENTH-CENTURY missionary Amy Carmichael who famously said, "You can give without loving, but you can't love without giving."

There are three primary ways that we give:

- Through our time
- Through our talents
- Through our treasure

Giving with Your Time

When Tara and I first started dating, I was attending a university located over two hours away from our hometown. She and I met and started seeing each other while I was home for summer break. It was expensive to have a long-distance relationship back then. Phone calls to a person living in another city weren't free. The phone company charged you by the minute. After I went back to school, the time away from her was painful. I was in love, so I didn't care how much the phone bill was. It turned out her parents did. They received a hefty phone bill from all of our phone calls that year. I would be missing her so much sometimes that I would finish a class at 2:00 p.m., I would get in my car and drive over two hours one way to be with her for two hours, and then I'd drive back to school that same day. Giving my time for her wasn't a chore. It was an honor.

A love relationship with God shouldn't be any different.

If a relationship has a high value in your life, you will make time for the relationship.

So many things are fighting for our time and attention. From serious things, like family and our jobs, to less serious things, like Netflix binging and video game playing.

Everyone and everything wants our time, so when we give our time to someone or something, we are making a big statement that we value this person or this thing.

I want you to recall what we already talked about when we talked about loving God with *all* of our souls. The most important thing that God wants is you. He wants to spend time with you. God has a dominant love language, and it's quality time.

Is God getting your time?

Maybe the way you can start spending more time with him is by waking up a little earlier in the morning to have what I call *Breakfast with Jesus*. Before you walk out the door, you make sure you sit with God for some time.

Another way you can make time with God a priority is by going out to a small group Bible study in the evening instead of staying home after a long day at work. You're exhausted from work, but you know it fills you every time you go to group. So you eat some dinner and head out the door to your small group to have a great discussion about Scripture and check in with your friends to see how they are holding up.

These are just two examples of how you can ascribe worth to God in giving your time to this very worthy relationship God has made available to you.

Giving with Your Talent

This may be a new concept for you. Giving your talent is where you can take your education, your experience, your skill set, your craft, or your trade, and you use it for the kingdom of God as a way of worshipping God.

In Exodus 36, we read about the people of God all coming to-gether to build the place of meeting. It reads in this chapter that "every skilled person to whom the Lord has given skill and ability" was called to help build the tent of meeting.

Imagine your skill set being used as an act of worship to help build the place of worship.

Here is the important question to ask:

How can I worship God with this talent that I've been given, this education I possess, this skill set I have acquired, this job ex-perience I have?

There is a way that you can take these things you have collected through the years and use them to ascribe worth back to God. This is what worship is all about.

I have so many friends who practice this form of worship.

My friend Jesse is a phenomenal car guy. He has been in the car world for decades and is one of the most networked guys I have ever met. He constantly has cars at his house from people he is helping out. Sometimes my car is one of them. If I have any issue with my car, if anyone in the church has any issue with their car, one call to Jesse, and it gets handled. The car will be fixed and back in your driveway, washed and repaired (at least he does this for his pastor). He does this because he told me it is a way he can give back for all God has done in his life. He's taking his skill set, and he's giving it back to God for God's kingdom. This is worship.

My friend Jared has been a producer in television for many years. He has helped put together some of the most-watched documentary shows on television. He is also deeply in love with Jesus. He now uses his talent to volunteer in our production booth, making sure our online content looks excellent, and he produces videos we play for our gatherings. This is worship.

My friends Trey and Ariel are gifted screenwriters and have created countless theater plays, musicals, and movies. They have taken their years of experience in the entertainment industry and now use it to make movies that elevate God. They've given their talent back to God as a way to show God the incredible value he has for their lives. This is worship.

My friend Brad has been in the financial world since he was sixteen years old. He now leads one of the largest financial management companies in our area. This man is gifted when it comes to money management. I am clueless about the financial world. Someone wanted to donate their stock to the church, so I called Brad. He told me that he had always wanted to use his education and experience with the financial world to help give back to the kingdom of God. He volunteered to help our church set up a whole system of how people can donate their stocks to the church. So if you have some stocks you've been feeling a nudge to donate, our church can now receive them. Feel free to visit our website for more information about that. Brad gave his talent to God as an act of worship.

My friend Shayley has had a heart for foster kids since she was very young. She became a certified foster care resource mom as a twenty-something single woman. Shayley began attending our church and shared a dream she had in her heart to open a home for teen girls in the foster care system who are pregnant. She knew this would be a big undertaking, but she felt she wanted to take her experience and use it to love these hurting teen girls with the love of Jesus. A year after Shayley shared this dream with us, someone donated a house, and Shayley is now a house mom for what we call "The Beverly," a home for teen girls in crisis. God is using Shayley as a healing hand of heaven for all of these girls. She gave her talent as an act of worship and God is now using it to rebuild lives.

I could go on and on and on with so many other friends using their talents in incredible ways.

I don't know your experience. I don't know your education, but have you ever thought about asking this question: "What can

I do to show value and ascribe worth to God through this talent in my life?"

After you ask the question, pray this prayer:

"Heavenly Father, show me a talent in my life I can use as a way to ascribe your worth to my life."

Then write down all the things that come to your mind. Choose one and go to your house of worship and ask them how you might use your talent to help build the house.

Giving with Your Treasure

This is probably the one way that you know the most about, but it is the hardest one to do for so many.

This is your money, your finances.

The most tangible way to ascribe worth and value to my relationship with God is by giving my money and financial resources to his kingdom.

As a pastor, I always get kind of embarrassed and awkward when I talk about giving to God financially because I think of how in times past, some pastors and church leaders have used talks about money to manipulate people, and because of that, some people have a jaded understanding about giving a financial offering to God.

As I read Scripture, especially the part about the early days of the church in the book of Acts, the people of God were passionate in the giving of their money and resources. Scripture tells us they would sell their personal property so they could give to anyone who had a need. Because of this kind of generosity, no one in the early days of the church had any needs. The church would have special offerings all the time to help struggling churches in other regions. The church had a reputation for being outrageously generous to all.

I believe this should still be the reputation of the church today. Unfortunately, now in our modern times, the church has lost this reputation. The way the church can start rebuilding its reputation is by its members worshipping God by giving their treasure. The more people give, the more ministry the church can do.

The truth is that ministry always costs money. Twice a year, our church sponsors a Serve Day, where we group up into different squads of people and deploy people around our community to do random acts of kindness, including projects like giving away free gas at local gas stations, hosting a free catered luncheon for the ER doctors and nurses at our local hospital, putting on a huge carnival for kids of families who are staying at a homeless shelter, repairing homes for the elderly, and so much more. We get quite a bit of stuff donated for the Serve Days, but these projects still cost the church quite a bit of money.

When people worship God through giving their treasure, the church can become outrageously generous to the community. I tell our church family this motto all the time. The more you give, the more we go.

Giving your money and your financial resources isn't just for the church to be generous. It's also for you to be blessed.

Remember: Jesus said, "Where your treasure is, there your heart will be also."

Taking this to mean your literal treasure, whatever you are investing in with your money will have your heart because your heart follows your treasure.

Your heart follows whatever you are investing in.

Years ago, our church took a small team to Africa where we helped a school and also held an evangelistic crusade. After a night where we saw some amazing miracles take place at the crusade, I caught a guy on our team checking his phone to see how his stock was performing back in the States. I was blown away that the awe of the miracles in Africa was lost to the price of a stock in America. He couldn't help himself because his affection was attached to his treasure.

This is why it is so important to ascribe worth to God by giving your treasure. By giving financially to the local church, you are making an investment, and this investment is going to cause your heart to follow. You will start getting more involved with the church as you begin investing in it. This is a blessing for you.

Jesus created the church as his body so that he could continue moving on the earth long after he was gone. The church is the vehicle Jesus empowered to bring heaven to earth. As you give financially to the church, you are in essence helping purchase the fuel for the vehicle God is using to change the world.

The more you give, the more the church goes.

There is another blessing that takes place when you give your treasure.

Scripture tells us there is a tangible blessing that happens for those who give a tithe of their treasure to the storehouse:

> "Bring the whole tithe into the storehouse, that there may be food in my house. Test me in this," says the Lord Almighty, "and see if I will not throw open the floodgates of heaven and pour out so much blessing that there will not be room enough to store it. I will prevent pests from devouring your crops, and the vines in your fields will not drop their fruit before it is ripe," says the Lord Almighty. "Then all the nations will call you blessed, for yours will be a delightful land," says the Lord Almighty. (MALACHI 3:10–12 NIV)

A *tithe* means "a tenth." This means that for those who choose to give 10 percent of their treasure to God's kingdom, there is a supernatural blessing that is unlocked for them. I call it God's heavenly boomerang effect. When you give the tithe, God turns around and gives back to you.

Some people have tried to convince me that the storehouse in this text can be any organization doing good things for God's kingdom, but I believe the New Testament equivalent to the Old Testament storehouse is the local church.

Here is the reality. If every person who calls himself or herself a follower of Jesus were to give 10 percent of their income to the local church, the local church would be able to do so many incredible things for their people and their community.

Imagine a church today where you walked in and no one in the church had any needs because the outrageous generosity of the people in the church allowed the church to be able to provide for the needs of every hurting person in the church.

In addition to creating an outrageously generous church, tithing unlocks a blessing for you. The benchmark for the blessing is giving at least 10 percent of your treasure. As you give your 10 percent, God opens the windows of heaven and gives you blessings, which then allows you to be even more generous.

In all my years of being a pastor, I have never had a person who faithfully tithed ever come to me and tell me they have a financial need in their lives. The people I know who faithfully tithe their treasure are incredibly blessed, including me.

Yes, I tithe. I have been faithfully tithing for decades now. I don't want to rob myself of the blessing God wants to pour into my life. I have personally experienced that you can't outgive God. The more I give, the more he seems to open the floodgates of heaven over my life, so more blessings flow to my life.

By the way, the blessings aren't necessarily in the form of more money in your bank account, even though that does happen sometimes. I have so many stories of ways God has blessed me that have nothing to do with money. Having three adult children who all love God and follow Jesus is the greatest blessing of all. Did tithing help make that happen? I believe it played a role because my kids all had front row seats to God supernaturally taking care of our family through some pretty crazy seasons.

One final thought about giving your treasure, more specifically, tithing your treasure. This Scripture in Malachi is the only place in the Bible where God says, "Test me." God is saying, "If you trust me with your treasure, I will supernaturally bless your 90 percent more than you could ever do with all 100 percent. Test me on this."

Worship Through Living

WORSHIP ISN'T JUST about what you do. Sometimes it's also about what you don't do:

> Therefore, I urge you, brothers and sisters, in view of God's mercy, to offer your bodies as a living sacrifice, holy and pleasing to God—this is your true and proper worship. (ROMANS 12:1 NIV)

Offering your body as a living sacrifice is what true and proper worship looks like.

During the sacrificial history period of Israel, the people of God would take animals, kill them, place them on an altar, and burn them as a way to worship God.

The imagery in this verse from Romans gives us a picture of placing on the altar any desires, affections, or passions that are not in alignment with God so they can be burned out of our lives as an act of worship to God.

In essence, when we die to living in ways that are ungodly, it is worship. We are ascribing worth to God and his kingdom when we tell our ungodly desires "no."

We live in a culture that has indoctrinated us with the exact opposite message:

"Don't tell yourself no."

"If you have desires, give yourself over to them because it is the only way to experience your true self."

A big way to worship God is to let those desires become a burnt offering to the Lord. God will be glorified, and you will be purified.

This isn't another form of legalism, where you are being mandated to quit doing certain things in order to go to heaven.

This is a form of sacrifice, where you are willingly giving something up to elevate God more in your life.

Here is a great prayer to pray every morning when you get up:

"Lord, show me anything in my life that I need to put on the altar that may be keeping me from being closer with You."

That's what any healthy relationship does. It eliminates all sources around it that could bring harm to the relationship and might be keeping the relationship from being more intimate.

For some reason, many people don't live their faith like this. Instead of evaluating what things in their lives to get rid of, they want to ask the question, "How far can I go or what bad things can I do before God finally says, 'That's it. I'm done with you. You're out!'"

Imagine having a marriage where you ask questions like, "How many people can I sleep with before my spouse actually leaves me?" or "How many times can I yell at my spouse before they get fed up with me and move out?"

No one who values a relationship in his or her life asks questions like that. Instead, they are asking questions like, "What can I purge from my life that will help bring me closer to this person and make my relationship with him or her better?"

And whatever that thing may be, a person who desires a healthy relationship will sacrifice that thing out of their life for the sake of a better relationship with that other person.

This is how we ought to be living in our relationship with God, continuously evaluating what things in our lives need to be purged so we can be closer to God.

This is what it means to be a living sacrifice as described in Romans 12.

Whether it's worship through singing, worship through giving, or worship through living, worship will be a vital part of keeping you from becoming blind to the blessing.

The blessing of God being in you.

The blessing of God moving for you.

The blessing of God working through you.

Strongholds of the Heart

THE SECOND MOST common reason some followers of Jesus have a struggle with loving God with *all* their hearts is the issue of strongholds of the heart.

A stronghold is defined as a place that has been fortified.

Whenever I hear the word *stronghold*, I picture the forts set up all over the United States back in the 1800s by the US Cavalry. These forts were built with large walls, bastions, and lookout towers to help keep the US Cavalry safe from attacks. Some of these forts are still standing to this day.

This is a great word picture of how a stronghold can form in your heart. It can start with some kind of unhealthy emotion as a result of a possible childhood or adolescent trauma. It can also start with an ungodly desire that wiggles its way in and roots itself deep in you. Either way, the emotion, or desire, drills down deep to anchor itself and starts building large walls to protect itself. These unhealthy emotions and desires continue to build up until they are fully protected with barriers to keep them from being removed.

Once the stronghold is securely in place within your heart, that's when the occupation begins. It moves from being an emotional problem to becoming a spiritual problem.

Throughout the Gospels, Jesus dealt with demonically possessed people. His disciples also had run-ins with the demonic. Paul, who wrote many of the letters in the New Testament, talks about the demonic realm quite a few times in many of his letters. I am not going to sugarcoat the truth. Demons were real in Bible times, and they are still around tormenting people today.

Just as the demonic realm uses thoughts to bring temptations, it is my belief and experience that the demonic realm also uses strongholds of the heart to begin occupying the heart. As soon as these entities occupy the heart, oppression begins.

Years ago, I witnessed a very seasoned believer in our church, who had an anger issue, begin to rage in anger at a meeting I was at. After the meeting, he had no recollection of what he had said or done while he was in a full rage. It's like something took over his body temporarily.

I have counseled multiple men who shared with me about their lust issues. They all seemed to tell me the same thing. "It was like lust took over my body and I no longer had control over what I did."

I have prayed with women who were so overwhelmed with anxiety and fear that they had uncontrollable shaking in their bodies.

The devil is an opportunist. He will use the strongholds of the heart to sneak in so he might begin to oppress your life.

By the way, oppression is much different from possession. As I understand Scripture, and from what I have personally experienced, a follower of Jesus who is filled with the Spirit of God cannot be possessed by a demonic entity. However, I do believe it is possible for a person who belongs to God and is filled with the Spirit to be oppressed by a demonic entity through a stronghold of the heart.

Possession takes place in the soul. Oppression takes place in the heart.

Here are some common signs of a demonic stronghold of the heart:

- Uncontrollable urges or desires
- Body shakes when you are overwhelmed with some kind of emotion
- Recurring nightmares
- Unexplained persistent physical sickness
- Unable to sit in a church gathering due to feeling anxious
- Unable to remember an emotional outburst or behavior

This is not an exhaustive list, but it gives you a good understanding of ways to help identify if a stronghold exists in your heart and if you are being oppressed.

When there are strongholds in your heart causing oppression in your life, it will make it virtually impossible for you to love God with *all* your heart.

Here is the good news. Scripture gives us guidance on how to deal with these strongholds:

> For though we live in the world, we do not wage war as
> the world does. The weapons we fight with are not the
> weapons of the world. On the contrary, they have divine
> power to demolish strongholds. (2 CORINTHIANS 10:3–4 NIV)

God has equipped you with different kinds of weapons to get rid of the strongholds of the heart.

This is called spiritual warfare.

The first step in demolishing the stronghold is identifying it and confessing it to another person you trust. There is something so cleansing and freeing in bringing darkness to light. The demonic realm doesn't like to be exposed. Demons do their best work in darkness. You render them powerless in your life by letting others know what's happening in your heart.

Once you have confessed the stronghold's presence in your heart, it's time to pray for God to clean your heart.

I would highly recommend going to a pastor or church leader to have them lay hands on you and pray for you. When you allow others to pray for you, God uses those prayers to uproot all the deep trenches the stronghold may have dug in your heart. Don't be surprised if you fall over as you are prayed for. It doesn't happen all the time, but many of the people I have prayed for that had a deep-rooted stronghold in their lives have fallen over after the stronghold was released from their hearts.

Once you have had others pray with you, I strongly recommend you get some counseling from a licensed Christian counselor to help you heal from the underlying trauma or the unhealthy desires and impulses you may have been experiencing. If you can't afford the counseling, find a local Celebrate Recovery group in your area and begin meeting weekly with the group to help with your healing and recovery.

Finally, I want to encourage you to keep clear of reintroducing your heart to what may have caused the stronghold to form in the first place. This could mean deleting some apps on your phone or deleting some relationships in your life. Once the heart has been healed and swept clean, it's imperative to guard it.

Remember the Scripture we covered earlier?

Above all else, guard your heart.

Scripture gives us a whole chapter devoted to instructing us on how to handle spiritual warfare. It's found in Ephesians 6:

> Finally, be strong in the Lord and in his mighty power. Put on the full armor of God, so that you can take your stand against the devil's schemes. For our struggle is not against flesh and blood, but against the rulers, against the authorities, against the powers of this dark world and against the spiritual forces of evil in the heavenly realms. Therefore put on the full armor of God, so that when the day of evil comes, you may be able to stand your ground, and after you have done everything, to stand. (EPHESIANS 6:10–13 NIV)

The best way to guard your heart against the strongholds from ever coming back is to make sure you suit up for battle every day. You will win this heart war because Jesus has already secured your victory.

The Heartbeat of God

Delight yourself in the Lord, and he will give you the desires of your heart. (PSALM 37:4 ESV)

MANY AMERICAN CHRISTIANS read this Scripture and interpret it to mean, "If I just hug God the right way or if I hit him at the right spot, he is like a cosmic vending machine. He will give me what I desire. I'll get what I want."

"Lord, I know that the desire of my heart is a cherry red Ferrari, so I know that a Ferrari is coming my way because I delight in you."

The reason we know this is not what this verse means is because this doesn't work.

God is not a genie in a bottle who gives us what we desire because we rub him the right way.

So what does this verse really mean?

Look at the language of what it's saying.

When you delight yourself in the Lord (that is, you are loving him with *all* of your heart, you are giving your heart *fully* and *completely* to God's kingdom), your heart gets close to God's heart. When your heart gets close to God's heart, your heart starts taking on the rhythm of his heart.

When this happens, God's desires start becoming your desires. God's passions become your passions.

What God loves, you begin to love.

What God despises, you despise.

What breaks God's heart breaks your heart.

As you delight yourself in the Lord, he gives you new desires for your heart and new passions for your life. His!

He recalibrates your old heart to get in rhythm and in sync with his heart.

This is why Scripture says that David was chosen by God because "he was a man after God's own heart."

David had the heartbeat of God.

Was he perfect? No.

God will use men and women who are imperfect but who have hearts moving in the same rhythm of his heartbeat.

If your heart is really in rhythm with God's heart, you're going to start feeling passionate for things you thought you'd never be passionate about.

I think of the story of Nehemiah from the Hebrew Scriptures. As he was in exile away from his homeland, working for the king of Persia, he was hit with some news from back home:

> They said to me, "Those who survived the exile and are back in the province are in great trouble and disgrace. The wall of Jerusalem is broken down, and its gates have been burned with fire." When I heard these things, I sat down and wept. For some days I mourned and fasted and prayed before the God of heaven. (NEHEMIAH 1:3–4 NIV)

He was so upset by this news he couldn't hide it from the king:

> So the king asked me, "Why does your face look so sad when you are not ill? This can be nothing but sadness of heart." I was very much afraid, but I said to the king, "May the king live forever! Why should my face not look sad when the city where my ancestors are buried

lies in ruins, and its gates have been destroyed by fire?"
(NEHEMIAH 2:2–3 NIV)

Nehemiah's heart was broken because God's heart was broken. The walls were knocked down, and the gates were burned, and God needed someone to rebuild the walls and restore the gates.

The work of rebuilding the walls and restoring the gates began when God first worked on the heart of someone who had a heart that *fully* and *completely* belonged to him. There are works of God that he wants to do in this world, but they're only going to be done and fulfilled by the people who have God's heartbeat.

I think of my own story with how we first started a ministry in Africa.

It started by watching TV one evening with my wife and kids. It was springtime, and I was planning our summer family vacation while watching a show called *American Idol*.

During the commercial breaks, I was running ideas by Tara on some options of where we could go and what we could afford to do for vacation. Then, as the show returned from one of the commercial breaks, something gripped my attention on the TV screen. The episode was called "American Idol Gives Back." The host, Ryan Seacrest, was in Africa and talking through the hardships one family was enduring. The camera crew followed a three-year-old who left his home to go hunting for something to feed the rest of his family. His father had died, leaving his mother on her own to care for him and his younger siblings. The little three-year-old found a den of baby rats and scooped them up to bring them back home so his family wouldn't starve.

As I was watching this on the TV screen, I looked down at my laptop screen to see all these places and prices for our vacation that we were planning. I began to weep. I quickly ran to my bedroom and closed the door behind me so my family wouldn't see me crying. I fell to the ground with my face in the carpet and began to sob uncontrollably. This was different from *The Little Mermaid* tears. It was the kind of cry where the snot was coming out of my nose in full force. I know that is TMI, but I need to tell you that detail to let you in on just how much I was being moved emotionally in that moment.

I even said out loud in my room, "What is happening to me?" I can't say I heard God audibly, but I heard him clearly. I heard these words, "You're crying my tears for my kids, and I'm activating you to do something about this."

Shortly after that encounter, I circled up with the leadership team at our church, and we went to prayer to find out where God was sending us. God led us to this beautiful couple in Zambia, Africa, who led a church and started a school for vulnerable and orphaned children. They educated the kids and fed them meals each day.

This amazing couple had been praying and believing that God would send them someone to help support them. They had no outside help and didn't have the resources to fill up the school and keep all the kids fed. God answered their prayers by activating me while watching *American Idol*. Thank you, Ryan! God used that show to give me his heartbeat for Africa.

We have now been partnering with these incredible people for over a decade. They now have a student enrollment of over eight hundred students with two campuses. Some of the students who graduated from our school continued their education and received teaching credentials. They are now employed and teaching at the very same school that helped them. It blows me away every time I think about it.

How did this all happen?

Because I delighted myself in the Lord and he gave me the desires, his desires, and infused them into my heart.

Let your heart beat for the things that God's heart beats for. And don't be surprised by the heavenly assignment that follows.

A Sobering Warning

A S WE FINISH this section about the heart, I want to end by giving you a sobering warning from Jesus himself.

During the first century, when Jesus was doing ministry in and around Jerusalem, there were these professional religious people called Pharisees. They had a reputation for being the most faithful followers of God.

They memorized the laws.

They obeyed the rules.

They knew the Torah.

They said their prayers.

They showed up at the synagogue on time.

They checked all the boxes religiously.

Yet Jesus called them out on so many occasions. He would call them names like snakes, brood of vipers, and fools.

Jesus did not mince his words at all against the Pharisees.

Why was Jesus so harsh with these seemingly perfect followers of God?

Even though they were saying all the right religious phrases and obeying all the right religious rules, Jesus understood their hearts were far from God.

In another conversation with these people, he quoted from the Hebrew prophet Isaiah:

> These people honor me with their lips, but their hearts are far from me. (MATTHEW 15:8 NIV)

Here's the truth:

This isn't just a warning for the Pharisees. This is a warning for all of us.

It's possible to go through all the motions and check all the boxes for what you should be doing as a follower of Jesus, and still have a heart that is far from God.

It's time for a heart check-up.

How is your heart beating these days for the things of God?

Do you get emotional at all when you start thinking about what God means to your life?

Can you remember the last time you really authentically worshipped God in some way?

What is something you have placed on the altar and sacrificed to help bring you closer to God?

Perhaps you feel more like the Pharisees of Jesus's time, just going through the motions of following Jesus without your heart involved at all?

Your desires determine your destiny, so don't settle for just going through the motions.

Get back to the heart of worship and your heart will be *full* of God.

The *greatest of all time* commandment is to love him with *all* of your being, and you can't do that without loving him with *all* your heart.

DISCUSSION QUESTIONS FOR PART 3:
All My Heart

- Reflect on a time when your emotions influenced your actions—whether positively or negatively. How did that experience shape your understanding of your heart's role in your life?

- This section emphasizes that God has a heart and experiences emotions. How does this truth affect your perception of God's nature and his relationship with you?

- What are some ways you can intentionally guard your heart daily to ensure it remains fully devoted to loving God?

- The section describes the heart as a *wellspring of life* and a *rudder* that directs your actions. How can you practically fill your heart with God's love and truth to influence your life positively?

- Have you ever experienced your heart being *deceived* or *manipulated* into wrong desires? What steps can you take to recognize and correct these influences?

- The story of King Asa's devotion versus King Abijah's lack of wholeheartedness illustrates the importance of heart commitment. In what areas of your life do you want to deepen your devotion to God?

- What are some *unhealthy affections* or desires that threaten to steer your heart away from God's purpose? How can you create spiritual security measures to protect against them?

- How does recognizing the vulnerability of your heart (as Jeremiah warns) motivate you to seek God's help in guarding your emotions and affections?

- In what ways can you cultivate a habit of regularly checking your heart to ensure it's aligned with loving God wholeheartedly?

- Reflect on how loving God with all your heart can impact your relationships, decisions, and future. What practical steps will you take today to love him more fully with *all* your heart?

PART 4

ALL MY STRENGTH

It is labor that keeps the strong man strong. And spiritual labor, toil and burden-bearing is what will give strength to the church of Christ.

—ELLEN G. WHITE

WELCOME TO THE final stop in this *greatest of all time* commandment.

We have already learned what it looks like to love God with *all* your soul, what it looks like to love God with *all* your mind, and what it looks like to love God with *all* your heart.

It's time to dive in and find out what it looks like to love God with *all* your strength.

For those of you who frequent the gym, despite what you may be thinking, loving God with *all* your strength doesn't mean doing a couple of extra reps on the bench press or throwing a few more plates on the squat rack.

Technically, that is strength, but when Scripture talks about strength, it means something so much more than just your sheer physical strength.

The Greek word used for *strength* in this *greatest of all time* commandment is *ischys* (pronounced is-khoos').

It means "ability, force, strength, might."

Another way we could say this part of the commandment is loving God with *all* of your *ability*.

The Hebrew word for *strength* gives us even more clarity to this word. The word is *meod* (pronounced meh-ode') and means "exceedingly, force, abundance, with muchness, with all your might."

A great expression that I believe captures the essence of this word is "putting it all on the line."

There is an epic story in the Hebrew Scriptures that really showcases this understanding of strength. It's found in the book of 2 Samuel.

First, a little context for this epic story.

David is waiting to be crowned king of Israel. Because the current king is hostile toward David, David is forced to live a life on the run, but as he was waiting for the crown, he started to collect his own following of men who believed in him and believed in his leadership. Scripture describes them as the "mighty men" of David. These dudes were a motley crew. They were really OG (abbreviation for "original gangsters"), but they loved David and would do anything for him. The Philistines, who were the enemy of Israel at the time, had conquered various territories around the area and protected them with squads of soldiers.

With that backstory in mind, listen to what these mighty men did for David:

> David longed for water and said, "Oh, that someone would get me a drink of water from the well near the gate of Bethlehem!" So the three mighty warriors broke through the Philistine lines, drew water from the well near the gate of Bethlehem, and carried it back to David. But he refused to drink it; instead, he poured it out before the Lord. "Far be it from me, Lord, to do this," he said. "Is it not the blood of men who went at the risk of their lives?" And David would not drink it. Such were the exploits of the three mighty warriors.
> (2 SAMUEL 23:15–17 NIV)

Think about what these men did.

They "put it all on the line" to fill David's "hydro flask."

They could have been killed for getting their bro a drink of water. That is some insane moxie.

These men loved David with *all their strength.*

As crazy as this act was, it doesn't surprise me, because when you love someone with your *all*, you will do just about anything for them.

Our love for God should be no exception.

When you love God with your *all*, you will be moved to do some radical things for him, just as you would be for anyone you love.

Here is a question that will help you assess where you are with this understanding of strength. What is the most radical thing that you have done in life, where you "put it all on the line" because of your love for God?

Maybe it was taking a trip overseas to share the love of God with a group of people you have never met.

Maybe it was boldly telling a coworker in the breakroom how God has transformed your life.

Maybe it was picking up some hitchhikers and offering them a ride to Vegas with you.

In my three-decade love affair with God, I have collected countless stories of radical acts I have felt moved to do.

One of my most memorable stories happened on one of my frequent road trips to Vegas. If you are wondering why I said frequent road trips, it's not because I have a compulsive gambling habit. I was part of a church plant there and would travel on the weekends to be the church's Sunday speaker. I racked up some serious miles on those trips to Vegas.

On one of these trips, I made my usual halfway point stop for coffee in the beautiful town of Barstow. As I exited the freeway, I saw two young guys flashing a sign asking for a ride to Vegas. Any resident of California knows people at off-ramps and intersections flashing signs asking for some kind of help is the norm. However, as I saw these two young men, I immediately felt the Spirit of God nudge me to offer them their free ride to Vegas. This is also when another voice started speaking into my mind: *What if these dudes have a gun and they are going to carjack you and kill you?* I know I have watched too many *Forensic Files* episodes to ignore that voice, so I called my wife to tell her what I was feeling God prompting me to do. She let me know her own concern about it, but then we prayed together on the phone.

Here was the prayer: "God, if this is of you, have those two young men still be there after I take a lap around the block. If these men are dangerous, send them away. In Jesus's name, amen."

After praying with my wife, I made the lap around the block and came back to the spot I had seen them at first. And, yes, they were still there. After my prayer with my wife, I was no longer concerned about the danger involved. I pulled up, rolled the window down, and with excitement in my voice, I shouted, "Hey, fellas, hop in! I'll give you a ride!" My enthusiasm probably gave these two their own concerns that they were the ones in danger.

They put their bags in my car and off we went to Vegas. I asked them some questions like, "Where are you guys from? Why are you going to Vegas?" They told me they were from Canada and were backpacking through America, on their way to stay at a hostel in Vegas. Then came the moment I had been waiting for. I explained to them I was a follower of Jesus and felt the Spirit of God prompt me to pick them up. I had two whole hours of being able to share with them the amazing ways God had changed my life and how God loves them so much he sent me to pick them up for a free Uber lift to Vegas.

Then, one of the two guys spoke up and said, "Before this trip, I had never heard about Jesus. Now, in one day, I have heard this same thing twice. The truck driver who gave us a ride to Barstow told us the same exact thing you just told us." They stopped short of praying with me to become followers of Jesus, but I asked them if I could pray over them before I dropped them off. They welcomed the prayer. I prayed a radical prayer that God would send them some more messengers to continue to show them how much he cares about them and has so much to offer their lives.

I have no doubt there were at least a few more messengers along their journey. I am grateful I was able to be one of them.

Here is the point of telling you this story.

When you love God with *all* your strength, these kinds of stories will be taking place in your life on the regular.

To get things done on earth as they are in heaven, God needs a body. Because you and I are part of the body of Christ, we have been anointed by God to be his hands, his feet, and his mouth to bring heaven to earth.

We are the only body God has to get things done, so it makes sense that he will prompt his followers into action.

Holy Spirit Activate

YEARS AGO, THERE was a viral video circulating on social media of Chynna Phillips from the '90s pop group Wilson Phillips. In the viral video, Chynna, who is a devout follower of Jesus, appeared on the game show *Family Feud* and interrupted the host Steve Harvey to sing her very own theme song before she did her final round of the game.

"Holy Spirit, activate!

"Holy Spirit, activate!

"Holy Spirit, activate, activate, activate!"

Say what you want about what she did. She and her team won that day. They did way better than our family did when we appeared on the show. I totally bombed on national TV, and our family lost the match. (I'll save that story for another time.) Who knows? Maybe there really was a supernatural activation through Chynna's song. In hindsight, I wish I had known that song before I appeared on the show. I could have used some supernatural help that day.

In all seriousness, I want you to know that when you are loving God with your *all*, there will be a true supernatural activation that takes place in you.

You aren't activating the Holy Spirit.

The Holy Spirit is activating you.

The Holy Spirit is the supernatural presence of God living in you as a believer:

> The Spirit of God, who raised Jesus from the dead, lives in you. And just as God raised Christ Jesus from the dead, he will give life to your mortal bodies by this same Spirit living within you. (ROMANS 8:11 NLT)

In essence, what this Scripture is talking about is possession. Some people prefer to use the word *indwelling*. I prefer the term *possession* because it helps me understand the concept better. (Maybe I prefer this term because of all the movies I watched in the '80s.)

As a believer in Jesus, you have been possessed by the Spirit of God, also referred to as the *Holy Spirit*, or as some denominations like to refer to him as the *Holy Ghost*.

The Holy Spirit is like the wind that hits your sails and causes your boat to get moving.

When you love God with *all* your strength, you won't be able to stay idle. You will be compelled to move.

This makes *strength* more like a verb rather than a noun.

Strength is your love for God in action.

Loving God with *all* your strength is a love that says, "God, I love you so much, I'm going to do something about it."

The letters from John are some of my favorite letters from Scripture. There is a running theme of love and action through all of them.

Look at this one verse in particular:

> My children, our love should not be just words and talk; it must be true love, which shows itself in action.
> (1 JOHN 3:18 GNT)

"True love" is not just saying something. It's doing something. Your actions give you away on how you are doing with loving God.

The book of James tells us our actions are a metric to measure not just our love for God but also our faith in God:

> But someone will say, "One person has faith, another has actions." My answer is, "Show me how anyone can have faith without actions. I will show you my faith by my actions." (JAMES 2:18 GNT)

Please hear what Scripture is teaching us.

This is not a call to *do* more. This is a call to *love* more, because when you love more, the *doing* will naturally and organically follow the *loving*.

To help you along in your activation, I want to cover what I feel are the three most significant ways to love God with *all* your strength.

1) Loving God Through Serving

ONE OF THE *greatest of all time* acts of Jesus happened just before he was killed. As he was at a dinner party held in his honor, Jesus shocked all the people in attendance by putting on a serving apron and washing all the feet of the guests in the room.

> When he had finished washing their feet, he put on his clothes and returned to his place. "Do you understand what I have done for you?" he asked them. "You call me 'Teacher' and 'Lord,' and rightly so, for that is what I am. Now that I, your Lord and Teacher, have washed your feet, you also should wash one another's feet. I have set you an example that you should do as I have done for you. Very truly I tell you, no servant is greater than his master, nor is a messenger greater than the one who sent him. Now that you know these things, you will be blessed if you do them." (JOHN 13:12–17 NIV)

Jesus, the Lord of Lords and the King of Kings, took on the job of foot washer, and said to his followers, "You do the same thing I just did."

I know some well-intentioned followers of Jesus who have taken this act of Jesus as a commission to literally go and wash people's feet.

Listen, I know these people mean well, but the act of foot washing itself wasn't the point Jesus was making.

For first-century dinner partygoers, a good foot washing would have been welcomed and much appreciated, especially considering no one wore closed-toed shoes and their main mode of transportation was walking. Those feet had to be mighty dirty.

If you try to wash people's feet in today's world, it just won't land the same way. People won't think you are serving them. They may actually think you have some kind of weird foot fetish.

Through this act of foot washing, Jesus was calling his followers to humble themselves, forget their reputations, and radically serve people.

Instead of foot washing, maybe a better comparable act in our modern world would be cleaning someone's bathroom or doing someone's laundry.

The idea Jesus is driving home is this: To be a true servant in God's kingdom, it's going to take a big bucket of humility. You are going to have to lower yourself to help lift others up, dirty feet and all.

This is the activation. Put on the apron, roll up your sleeves, and go serve someone.

By doing so, you will be putting your love in action, and according to Jesus, you will also be promoted to greatness in God's kingdom:

> Whoever wants to become great among you must be your servant, and whoever wants to be first must be your slave—just as the Son of Man did not come to be served, but to serve, and to give his life as a ransom for many. (MATTHEW 20:26–28 NIV)

Jesus modeled this servanthood for two different groups of people.

As you read in the foot-washing episode, Jesus served his followers, the people who were with him. These were the people actively doing life with him. Even though he was their leader, the Gospels give us example after example of ways Jesus would put them before himself.

In addition to serving the people with him, Jesus also served the people around him. People he encountered along the path of his travel. People he had no prior relationship with. Jesus served them by healing them, delivering them, and even at times feeding them.

I want you to know, you are most like Jesus when you are serving people, and just as Jesus served two groups of people in his life, you also have these same two groups of people in your life:

People around you.

People with you.

First, let me share with you about the people around you.

These are the people you work with. These are the people that you live by.

These are the people that you shop at the grocery store with.

You may not know their first names, but they're around you.

Second, there are the people with you.

These are people you are very acquainted with.

This group would include your family.

This group would also include your very close friends, otherwise known as your BFFs. This group would also include the people who you attend church with. We call these people our brothers and sisters in Christ. This is your faith family.

Just as Jesus was activated to serve both groups of people, when you are loving God with your *all*, you should also experience an activation to serve both groups of people in your life.

The People Around You

When my kids were little, we loved to take them down to San Diego for family vacations every year. One of our favorite places to go was SeaWorld. (Sorry if you're not a fan of SeaWorld. Don't judge us.) At the dolphin show, a singer would always perform a few songs before the show began. One of the songs is specifically sung to warn all the guests sitting in the first several rows in the arena that they are going to get soaked during the show. They refer to these rows as the "splash zone."

I like to think of the *people around you* as the people close enough to you that your life is going to splash on them in some way. You don't necessarily know them or have any relationship with them, but they are close enough to you to get soaked by your servanthood.

Divine Appointments

Every day, our lives involve people to some degree. I have learned to look at all my random encounters with other humans as not random at all. I choose to look at every person who crosses my path as a possible divine appointment set up by God. I truly believe "the steps of a righteous person are ordered by God" (Psalm 37:23). So, I choose to believe God places me with people for a purpose.

Every time I leave my house in the morning, I can faintly hear the theme song of the movie *Mission: Impossible* playing in the background, leaving me with an adventurous question in my mind: *What heavenly mission awaits me today?*

It makes life so much more fun to view people this way, and it also creates a great opportunity to splash some heavenly love on people around me who are in desperate need of it.

How about you?

Have you ever considered the possibility that God has placed the people around you on purpose for a purpose?

What if it wasn't your impressive resume that landed you the job, but rather it was a divine intervention by God because he needed you at that company to be there to give some godly advice to the vice president who is going through a divorce?

What if your loan actually was approved for the mortgage on your house, not because of your good credit, but because God intervened due to a neighbor living next door who has been struggling with suicidal thoughts? And God knows you will speak life to them, pray with them, and they will be healed of their issues in the process.

What if you lived as if there are no such things as coincidences, but only divine providences when it comes to your close encounters with other humans?

I have heard a mantra for years. I don't know who originally said it. I have heard it said from many different pastors and leaders. All I know is I am glad I heard it, because I have adopted it as a way to help activate me in how I might effectively serve the people around me. Now I want to pass it on to you.

Find a need and fill it.

Find a hurt and heal it.

Find a Need and Fill It

Here's what I know about the people around you.

Most of them have a need.

Maybe someone at work told you about something happening to their family.

Maybe a neighbor on your street shared with you something going on in their life.

As you think about what they shared with you, the first thought that should cross your mind is, *How can I help them with this need?*

Maybe you have the extra resources.

Maybe you have the capabilities to actually take care of that need.

When you fill a person's need, you are being a servant to that person.

Years ago, when I was leading a church in Las Vegas, I was moved with compassion for the people who lived around the neighborhood where our church was located. When I was doing my drive-through prayer around the neighborhood, I witnessed a lot of brokenness in the people I saw walking around. As I processed what I witnessed around our neighborhood, I felt an opportunity was being revealed to me. Our church came together and created an outreach that we named Adopt-a-Block. Our church would go house to house, seeing if there was anything we could do to serve them in practical ways. We had so many life-changing encounters with our neighbors because we stepped up and filled some needs they had. Many people in this same neighborhood are now followers of Jesus and actively a part of our church community because we took the initiative to help fill some needs for them.

Find a Hurt and Heal It

After leading this amazing inner-city church in the city of Las Vegas for ten years, my wife and I were surprised when God supernaturally called us to a city we had never heard of—Thousand Oaks, California.

What made this so surprising to us was that this city and the cities surrounding it are part of one of the most affluent areas in the United States.

According to *Forbes* magazine, the Los Angeles area is ranked as the sixth most expensive place to live in the world.[25] (Thousand Oaks happens to be included in this area.)

The reason I point this out is because I came to the area with a preconceived idea that money would stamp out a lot of people's hurt because they wouldn't be struggling with all the stuff I saw so many people struggling with in Vegas. But instead, to my surprise, I have experienced way more hurting people in Thousand Oaks than I ever experienced in Vegas.

Have you ever heard the expression, "Mo' money, mo' problems"?

Here's the hard truth.

Money cannot heal a hurt.

Despite their nice homes or the new cars in their driveways, there are some hurting people you're living next to.

There are some hurting people who you're working with.

There are some hurting people who are literally standing right next to you at the gas pump.

A few years ago, I pulled into a gas station to fill up my car on a hot Vegas night. As I started filling up my car, I felt like I was supposed to pray for someone at the gas station, but no one was there besides me. So I decided to pray a specific prayer. "Lord, if this is you, cause someone to pull up right next to me directly on the other side of my gas pump, then I'll know it's You." As soon as I finished praying this prayer, a car pulled up. There were eleven empty gas pumps. You can probably guess which one they pulled up to. A woman got out of the car and started to fill her car up. That's when I awkwardly peeked around the pump and told her I was a pastor at a church, and I had just felt God speak to me that someone would be getting gas next to me who needed prayer. I asked if she believed in God, and when she said yes, I asked if I could pray for her. I can't recall the exact prayer I prayed over her, but I will never forget those tears. She hugged me and told me I would never understand what that meant to her. This all happened as I was simply getting some gas for my car.

My wife has a saying that she often reminds me of, especially after we deal with a grumpy person out in public: "Everyone is fighting a battle you know nothing about, so always be kind."

I need to be reminded of that, not just for the times I deal with grumpy people. I need to be reminded of that at all times.

Whether it's filling a need or healing a hurt, I am convinced we would be experiencing more miracles of God in our lives if we actually served the people around us.

This is a big reason why our church does an all-church Serve Day twice a year. We take four hours on a Saturday to squad up on different projects to show some *no-strings-attached, Jesus-style love.*

These Serve Days help show our church just how easy it is to be used by God, and bring healing and hope to someone's life.

In addition to our Serve Days, our church started doing a community project called the Plus One Challenge. A few times a year,

I encourage the church to bring a dollar bill to a Sunday gathering and place it in a special box called the Plus One Box. This money is used to bless a random person in our community. The first time we did this, we brought in a thousand dollars. After changing out the one-dollar bills to hundred-dollar bills, I took one of our other leaders with me to go find the person we felt God wanted us to give it to.

After we prayed, we both felt a nudge that we were supposed to bless a worker at one of our local fast-food restaurants. We went to the drive-through lane, ordered drinks, and pulled up to the window. I told the woman working the window thanks for the drinks and that I now had something to give to her. I pulled the envelope out with a thousand dollars cash and said, "This is for you." I told her I was a pastor of a local church and that God directed us to the drive-through to bless her. The woman broke out in tears. She proceeded to tell me her rent was due, and she didn't have the money to pay it, and then we happened to show up. We couldn't stay long in the drive-through with people waiting behind us, but I had just enough time to tell her how much God loves her and cares deeply about her, so much that he sent two dudes in a drive-through to make sure her rent was paid. We then prayed over her and drove off.

Miracles are waiting to happen all around you. The only thing needed to ignite the miracle is your willingness to "put it all on the line" and begin serving the people around you.

The People with You

The second group of people Jesus served well were the people near him, primarily the people who were doing ministry with him. The best way to describe this group of people is "family."

Have you ever been invited to another family's home for dinner and witnessed what it looks like when the whole family pitches in and helps out, including the little ones?

When the dinner is finished, without a parent saying a word, the kids get up and start taking the dishes to the sink. You watch as one child takes the full trash can outside to empty it. Another child starts wiping the counters down.

I've seen this a few times from families we have visited for dinner, and it is so impressive to watch.

When everyone is active, when everyone is contributing, when everyone is serving, it makes for a functional family.

If all of the household responsibilities are on one person or just the parents, and the rest of the family members aren't contributing, it creates an unhealthy household where one person is overwhelmed while the other people in the house are sitting on the couch watching Netflix.

The church is not a building. It's a body. It's a family. People coming together to share life with one another.

In order for the church to be a functional family of God, everyone must contribute. When everyone in the family has the posture of serving one another, just as Jesus demonstrated, the church is able to do everything God intends it to do.

You Have Superpowers

The great part about serving the people with you, especially your church family, is that God has equipped you with supernatural power to do it.

Scripture tells us part of the benefit of being filled with the Spirit of God is that we receive supernatural gifts, often referred to as "spiritual gifts" in the New Testament Scriptures.

When you received the Holy Spirit, God gave you some abilities that you didn't have prior to being saved. We have different gifts, according to the grace given to each of us:

> If your gift is prophesying, then prophesy in accor-
> dance with your faith; if it is serving, then serve; if it

is teaching, then teach; if it is to encourage, then give encouragement; if it is giving, then give generously; if it is to lead, do it diligently; if it is to show mercy, do it cheerfully. (ROMANS 12:6–8 NIV)

A great working definition of a spiritual gift is the special supernatural ability to excel at a certain action in your faith that ultimately can be used to serve the church in order to make it stronger and more effective:

God has given each of you a gift from his great variety of spiritual gifts. Use them well to serve one another. (1 PETER 4:10 NLT)

The purpose of God giving you these supernatural gifts is so you can serve the people with you, especially his church.

I know this is a weird word picture, but imagine God having a kitchen pantry in heaven. Imagine him for a moment going into the pantry with a big scooper in hand. He goes for the canister on the shelf marked with the word *faith* written on it. Instead of taking only one scoop from the canister, he decides to take an extra scoop and then pours both scoops into you. This is what it's like to receive a spiritual gift.

Every follower of Jesus has faith, but there are some followers who I have witnessed who seem to have been given an extra scoop of it. They are able to trust God in ways most people can't.

Everyone should be able to share the Gospel with other people. This is often called *evangelism* in the church. But some people seem to have been given an extra scoop of *evangelism* from heaven. They share about Jesus with such ease and power.

Everyone can talk through a Bible passage, but I have witnessed some people who seem to have been given an extra scoop of *teaching* and have this special ability to explain things about Scripture in ways no one else can.

Every follower of Jesus is called to help out and participate in the church, but there are some followers who seem to have received a little extra scoop from heaven on their ability to *help*. These followers help out with such excitement and ease. You would almost think they had some special supernatural training for it.

The best way to describe these people who seem to have been given an extra scoop of some spiritual ability is that they are gifted.

I want you to know that God has not left you out. As a Spirit-filled follower of Jesus, you also have received an extra scoop of some kind of ability in your life for the sake of serving the people with you.

The apostle Paul writes about these spiritual gifts quite a bit in the letters he wrote to the various churches. Some of the places in Scripture where you can find these spiritual gifts listed by name are Ephesians 4, Romans 12, and 1 Corinthians 12.

The church in Corinth seemed to have some struggle understanding how to properly use their spiritual gifts to serve the church. To help the Corinthians understand how spiritual gifts are supposed to be used to serve the church, the apostle Paul uses the analogy of a body to describe the church:

> Just as a body, though one, has many parts, but all its many parts form one body, so it is with Christ. (1 CORINTHIANS 12:12 NIV)

> Even so the body is not made up of one part but of many. (1 CORINTHIANS 12:14 NIV)

> Now you are the body of Christ, and each one of you is a part of it. (1 CORINTHIANS 12:27 NIV)

For a body to be functional, all the parts have to be working. All the parts have to contribute. If they don't, we would call the body dysfunctional.

The church is the body of Christ.

In order for the church to be a functional body, every body part must work together with the other parts and contribute. This requires everyone who is part of the body to be activated to serve.

This is why there is a real challenge in the American church right now.

Most Americans are conditioned to having other people serve them.

We go to a restaurant; we're served.

We go to watch a game; we're served.

We're served so much that it is almost a built-in expectation that people will be with us to serve us.

Unfortunately, this attitude has spilled over into many people's attitudes toward how they view the church.

How can the church serve me?

What can the church do for me?

Cue the famous President Kennedy speech (with a slight modification):

> Ask not what your church can do for you. Ask what
> you can do for your church.

As you read through Scripture, you will see with spectacular clarity that you have been called by God to be a contributor in this great movement called the church.

The church cannot fully be all that God has called it to be without you actively being part of it.

And you can't be all God wants you to be without you actively being part of his church.

For a follower of Jesus to say, "I don't need to be part of a church" is like a kidney saying, "I don't need a body to function."

You need the church and the church needs you.

You are called to contribute to the family and God has gifted you so you can help the body of Christ be all it has been called to be.

Discovering Your Gift

> Everyone is gifted, but some people never open their package.
> —*Wolfgang Riebe*
> (GERMAN BORN ACTOR AND ENTERTAINER)

Have you opened your package?

Do you know what your spiritual gift is?

When I hear, "loving God with your strength," very often I think of loving God with your "strengths."

In the business world, it seems there are continually new assessment tests that companies have their employees take in order to help their organizations run more efficiently and hire more proficiently. From the Myers-Briggs to the new trending Enneagram, it seems there are quite a few ways to assess your strengths these days.

Just like you can find all kinds of personal strength assessments online, you can also find lots of spiritual gift assessments online. Just google "spiritual gift assessment," and you will have hundreds of assessments to choose from.

As fun as it is to take assessments and go over the results with a friend, it's not a 100 percent accurate way to discover your spiritual gifts. I have taken lots of these assessments over the years, and it seems every time I have taken one, I have had different results.

Even though I am a fan of taking these spiritual gift assessments, I believe the only way you can fully understand how God has gifted you and equipped you to be a servant for the body of Christ is by actually stepping up and serving in some capacity.

The best place to start serving is in the area you think you may have been given an extra scoop to contribute. Choose to look at it as the lab portion of your class in spiritual gifts. You are going to discover your gift through experimentation.

There are two major markers that will help you discern what your extra scoop is and how you have been gifted to serve and contribute to your church family.

Your Gift Will Fuel You

A great way to know you are serving in an area you have been gifted by God for is by paying attention to what I call your internal life-giving meter. If you serve in some way and your experience is life-giving to you, it may be a sign you are serving in the right spot.

Maybe it's serving by greeting people?

Maybe it's working the computers in the tech booth?

Maybe it's helping take care of the kids?

Some people are gifted for teaching kids. They serve in kids' ministry and leave their volunteer shift saying, "Wow! There's nothing more heavenly for me than listening to a three-year-old talk and teach them about God." Whereas another person may volunteer for the same shift and leave thinking, "Being in a room with thirty preschoolers is not like heaven. It's more like hell." For the person who thinks that way, volunteering to teach little kids is probably not where God has wired them to be. It's not life-giving for them. It's life-taking. Listen to your internal life-giving meter.

Your Gift Will Feed Others

When you step into a serving role in the church and other people in the church begin to give you positive feedback, it's another sign you are probably serving in an area you are gifted for. When people begin telling you things like, "What you did really impacted me. What you said really inspired me," you are probably serving in the role God has gifted you for.

However, if you love serving in a position but there doesn't seem to be much feedback coming your way, it may be a sign that you are not operating in your gifting.

There was an amazing man who attended our church years ago who had such a desire to teach middle school students. He loved Jesus and was so passionate about Scripture. However, when he taught the middle school students, they were bored out of their minds. Parents began calling the church, asking if we could find another person to teach the students. I felt so bad for this guy because I knew how much he loved to teach. He just wasn't gifted for it. However, this same man would come to a Sunday gathering and tell me how he had led several middle school students to the Lord at the local skate park over the weekend. He may not have had the gift of *teaching*, but he most definitely had the gift of *evangelism*.

Pay attention to all the feedback, the good, and maybe the not-so-good. It's going to help point you to the position God has gifted you to serve in.

God's Benefit Package

The people *around* us and the people *with* us both have this in common: They get blessed when we serve them.

Not only do the people you serve get blessed, according to both Scripture and science, you also get blessed when you serve others:

> Those who refresh others will themselves be refreshed.
> (PROVERBS 11:25 NLT)

I call this God's *blessing boomerang*.

As you step out to serve and encourage someone, the encouragement boomerangs right back to you.

Science has once again caught up with what Scripture has been telling us for thousands of years.

Studies in both neuroscience and psychology have now discovered that your body releases the "feel-good" chemical dopamine, and in some cases oxytocin, when you serve other people. These are the same "feel-good" chemicals your body releases when you are eating food or being physically intimate with your spouse. This phenomenon is now commonly referred to as the "helper's high."[26]

Isn't it crazy to think your brain has a built-in reward system for when you serve others? I would go as far as to say that God has pre-wired you to serve others, and he wants to make you feel so good doing it that you will want to do it again and again.

Depression is a very complex issue, and I, by no means, would ever want to come across like I am oversimplifying the cure, but study after study I have read has shown people who struggle with depression see a reduction in their own depression as they serve other people.

I have had plenty of days when I felt there was a dark cloud over me. I will tell you from my own personal experience that one of the fastest ways to get rid of those dark clouds above you is to serve other people in some way.

I know I am at my best when I am serving others.

Serving blesses people around me.

Serving blesses people with me.

Serving even blesses me.

And then one more good reason to serve people:

Serving keeps me from swerving.

The more I help others, the more I see God using me, the less likely I am to veer off track in my life.

I know so many people who claim to be followers of Jesus, but are completely inactive when it comes to doing anything to serve people.

I want you to know inactivity is your enemy.

People who become bored with their lives tend to slip backward in their faith.

Make a decision to live like Jesus by serving like Jesus.

Not only will it make a difference in a person's life that you serve, but also, it will also make a big difference in you.

One final thought about serving others.

If you feel unqualified to serve people, you are not alone. I feel this all the time, but as I read Scripture, it makes me feel more at ease with this feeling of inadequacy. The Bible is filled with example after example of God using unqualified people in supernatural ways to make a difference in this world.

2) Loving God Through Sharing

WHEN YOU ARE loving God with *all* your strength, another way you will be activated is through sharing this relationship you have with God with other people.

We do this with everything we love.

Have you ever tried a new restaurant out and had the best food you have ever eaten? One of the first things you do is you begin sharing your experience with your family and friends, those people who you love. You want them to experience what you experienced.

We do this with Netflix series we have enjoyed, places we have visited, books we've read.

We want to share our loves with the people we love.

Your love for God ought to be no different.

In his final words to his followers before he leaves this world, Jesus commissions them to share the Good News wherever they go. This is commonly referred to as the Great Commission:

> Then Jesus said to them, "So wherever you go in the world, tell everyone the Good News." (MARK 16:15 GW)

What's the *Good News?*

> For God so loved the world that he gave his one and only Son, that whoever believes in him shall not perish but have eternal life. (JOHN 3:16 NIV)

Even though you've blown it, even though you've made mistakes, Jesus still died for you and forgave you so that he can empower you to live differently, to live more heavenly in your life.

Jesus said wherever you go, share this with people.

Sharing your relationship with God to other people can feel quite intimidating. After all, eternity is at stake.

What if I mess it up and don't share it correctly?

What if they ask me a question I don't know the answer to?

What if I freak them out and they don't want anything to do with me anymore?

I had all these "what-ifs" myself.

In addition to these what-ifs, I also had concerns that I didn't know enough about the Bible.

It is so easy to overthink this idea of sharing your relationship with God with other people. You can overthink it so much that you can talk yourself out of saying anything about it to anyone.

Through the years, I have learned different methods of sharing my faith, like the Romans Road or the Four Spiritual Laws. I have memorized certain key verses to help people understand why they need a relationship with God. I have even practiced sharing my faith with other believers to get more comfortable with it. None of these methods are bad. In some ways, they can be quite helpful, but I think by focusing so much on the "how to," you can miss the beauty of the simplicity of just sharing your personal experience of how a relationship with God changed your life. I call this your own personal short story.

One of the greatest stories in Scripture that helped me overcome my propensity to overthink what it looks like to share my faith is found in the book of Acts:

> Then Peter stood up with the Eleven, raised his voice and addressed the crowd: "Fellow Jews and all of you who live in Jerusalem, let me explain this to you; listen carefully to what I say." (ACTS 2:14 NIV)

> With many other words, he warned them; and he pleaded with them, "Save yourselves from this corrupt generation." Those who accepted his message were baptized, and about three thousand were added to their number that day. (ACTS 2:40–41 NIV)

These men were in the upper room, scared and concerned about what might happen to them if people found out they were followers of Jesus. Once the Spirit of God got hold of them, their whole demeanor changed.

Peter shared his heart, and about three thousand people became followers of Jesus that day.

It wasn't some method he had memorized. It wasn't a speech he had rehearsed. It was a Spirit-filled moment where Peter opened his mouth and shared about a man who changed his life.

Again, I know there are so many methods out there about "how to" share your faith, but I want to really simplify it for you.

The most powerful thing you can share with someone about your faith in God is your personal experience with God.

Maybe you have never thought about your own story before.

Let me help you with it.

Start by looking at your relationship with God as a short three-chapter book.

Chapter 1: My Life Before Jesus

Everyone has an origin story.

What was your life like before Jesus?

Whether it's sharing about your time in prison, or the way your parents raised you in the church, we all have a past.

Start there.

Be willing to share your scars.

Being authentic and transparent is the best way to have people connect with you.

Don't get too detailed with this chapter of your story. Think of it as a quick flyover chapter. Most of your time should be spent on the next two chapters.

Chapter 2: My Life when I Gave It to Jesus

How was your life radically changed with Jesus?

Maybe it was a prayer you prayed after a church gathering, and you were filled with an indescribable peace.

Maybe God delivered you of some kind of addiction.

Maybe you were able to finally forgive someone from a past hurt.

Chapter 3: My Life Now That I Am Giving My All to God
What is happening in your life because you are following Jesus?

What ways have you seen following Jesus help your life?

This chapter is where you share the incredible things God is at work doing in your life now that Jesus is leading your life.

Even if you have been following Jesus since you were five years old, you ought to have some examples of amazing things God has done for your life by having Jesus lead your life.

I refer to these events as "God stories."

It could be how God restored your marriage.

It could be how God healed you of an illness.

It could be how God supernaturally provided for you through a tough financial situation you were in.

The great news is your chapter 3 is still being written.

Before your life is over, you will be adding so many more stories to this chapter.

I WANT TO encourage you to write out your story.

Writing it out will help you summarize it. The ideal scenario is to be able to share your whole story, all three chapters, in five minutes.

Once you write it out, practice sharing your story with a few friends so you get more comfortable with telling it.

Sharing your story with someone is going to benefit not only the person you are sharing it with but also you.

Every time you share your story, you are reminding yourself of just how amazing it is to follow Jesus.

Another great benefit of sharing your own story is that no one can argue against your own personal experience.

People may be able to debate you on some other facts of Christianity, but they won't be able to debate your own story.

As far as not feeling knowledgeable enough about the Bible, or not being able to answer all the questions people may throw at you, I want to remind you that you are living in the information age.

As you are sharing with someone, and they have a question that you don't know how to answer, don't be intimidated to tell them you don't know the answer to their question. Do a web search for the answer to their question and walk through the answer with them.

One website I have learned to really appreciate in my adventures of sharing my faith with other people is gotquestions.org. This website has biblical responses to literally thousands of questions.

An Open Invitation

Of course, one of the easiest ways to open up a conversation about your relationship with God to someone is to simply invite them to attend a weekend gathering with you at your local church.

I call this the *come and see* method.

There are so many people in our church who are now followers of Jesus because a friend or family member simply invited them to *come and see* how God is real and how he wants to change their lives. They accepted the invitation and attended a weekend gathering. Then God met them in a supernatural way while they were listening to the music or hearing the speaker talk about God. A simple invitation changed their lives.

You might feel a little intimidated to share your faith with someone, but what I want you to consider is the strong momentum of heaven already moving in that person's life.

God speaks to people all the time in different ways. When you share your faith with someone, you never know how God has already been working on that person's life before you came along. You opening up and sharing with them may be the final confirmation they need to give their life to God.

Just like Peter, let the Spirit of God lead you all the way through the process of sharing your faith, including who it is you are supposed to share with.

One of the strangest times I had a prompting to share my faith with someone was with a guy hitting it hard on the stair climber machine in the corner of the gym I work out at. I was getting a great workout in myself and as I was on the elliptical machine, I felt the Spirit of God take the mic in my mind and say, "That guy needs a messenger right now. Go over and talk with him, and let him know I sent you to him." I look over and this guy is dripping in sweat. He is in the middle of a hard workout. I tried to ignore the prompting, but it got even louder, so I knew I was being sent to this guy.

I went over to where he was, jumped on the machine next to him, and started talking with him. I don't recall exactly what I said, but it went something like this.

"Hey, bro! I'm a Christian, and I just felt compelled to come over here. I don't know what's going on with your life, but I feel like God sent me over here as a messenger for you. I know you are in the middle of a hard workout, so I don't want to interrupt you, but just know God loves you. He died for you. And whatever you are going through, you can give it to him, and he is going to help you."

After I finished telling him this, he looked at me intently and said, "Wow! You have no idea what this means to me. I needed to hear this right now." He told me, "Thank you so much." And that was it. He kept climbing the stairs. I gave him a fist bump and went back to my workout.

I don't know if he was already a follower of Jesus and God sent me to him to confirm something for him. Or maybe he had just prayed and said, "God, if you're real, send me a message somehow." Believe it or not, I hear from people quite a bit who have prayed a prayer just like that, and the people I have heard it from have told me a random person came up to them and shared their faith with them.

I am convinced, if you listen close enough, you will hear the Spirit of God direct you to someone as well.

In order for people to hear the message, God sends his kids to tell them:

> How, then, can they call on the one they have not believed in? And how can they believe in the one of whom they have not heard? And how can they hear without someone preaching to them? And how can anyone preach unless they are sent? As it is written: "How beautiful are the feet of those who bring good news!" (ROMANS 10:14–15 NIV)

God may be sending you to be a messenger for someone who is right on the verge of believing in God, and you may be the final confirmation they need to give their life to God.

If you focus more on God's great love for that person and his ability to do great things for their life, rather than on how you might come off looking like a weirdo, you'll be more motivated to share with them.

God may use your words to change their life forever.

3) Loving God Through Subduing

T**HE THIRD WAY** of loving God with *all* your strength doesn't involve any action at all. It actually is about inaction.

Loving God with *all* your strength will sometimes call for your *restraint*.

Like an athlete preparing for a big competition, there are just some things you need to avoid doing in order to be able to perform at your best.

Scripture actually uses this analogy:

> Do you not know that all the runners in a stadium compete, but only one receives the prize? So run to win. Each competitor must exercise self-control in everything. They do it to receive a perishable crown, but we an imperishable one. So I do not run uncertainly or box like one who hits only air. Instead I subdue my body and make it my slave, so that after preaching to others I myself will not be disqualified. (1 CORINTHIANS 9:24–27 NET)

"I subdue my body and make it my slave."

To *subdue* means to bring under control.

This is completely countercultural to what we are used to hearing in our modern world.

Terms like "YOLO" (You only live once) and "DIFTP" (Do it for the plot) are the mantras most people live by these days.

"If it feels good, do it" seems to be the way most people choose to live their lives.

It's interesting to note that one of the chief principles of modern-day Satanism is the mantra originally coined by the twentieth-century occultist Aleister Crowley: "Do whatever thou wilt shall be the whole of the law."[27]

Doing whatever feels good in the moment or doing whatever you desire are terrible ways to live your life, whether you follow Jesus or not.

Many impulses and desires we have stand in complete opposition to living a healthy life. If we were to give our bodies over to every impulse and desire we have, not only would it be impossible to live out the life God has purposed us to live, we would probably live a much shorter life.

Subduing the body becomes a necessity to live the life God has for you.

Listen to what Jesus says to his own disciples:

> Then Jesus said to his disciples, "Whoever wants to be my disciple must deny themselves and take up their cross and follow me." (MATTHEW 16:24 NIV)

To get the church in Corinth to understand loving God with *all* your strength involves telling your body *no* sometimes, Paul wrote this:

> You say, "I am allowed to do anything"—but not everything is good for you. You say, "I am allowed to do anything"—but not everything is beneficial.
> (1 CORINTHIANS 10:23 NLT)

There will be moments you're going to experience as a follower of Jesus where you will be able to demonstrate your love for God by not giving in to the impulses or desires your body may have.

I'm not going there.

I'm not doing that.

Why?

It's not because I can't. I live in a free country. I'm allowed to do a lot of things, as long as they aren't illegal.

But I know by doing that thing, going to that place, being with that person, I'm actually drawing myself away from my relationship with God.

My body wants to.

My body desires to.

However, it's not good for me.

However, it's not beneficial for me.

Therefore, I am going to pass.

Can you imagine a professional athlete downing a big slice of cheesecake right before a competition just because he or she had a craving for it?

Athletes will say *no* to some things that they may crave or desire for the greater reward of winning the competition.

There are so many things in this world that are going to appeal to your desires. They will look so good to you, but you also know they aren't good for you. They actually weigh you down and make it more difficult to love God with your *all*.

Here is another great athletic metaphor from Scripture:

> Therefore, since we are surrounded by such a great cloud of witnesses, let us throw off everything that hinders and the sin that so easily entangles. And let us run with perseverance the race marked out for us. (HEBREWS 12:1 NIV)

There are things you may be doing that are weighing you down, making it so much more difficult to run the race God has marked out for you.

I could give you a laundry list of things that Scripture tells you explicitly to avoid doing, things that you can do with your body that can harm you and even potentially kill you.

Knowing that giving in to certain impulses and desires can be harmful to me has changed how I read Scripture. When I see a command in the Bible telling me to avoid something, I no longer think of it as God trying to spoil my fun. Instead, I see it as God looking out for my well-being. So, whenever I read a *don't* in Scripture, I understand it as God saying, "*Don't* hurt yourself."

Instead of going down the whole list of don'ts, I want to simplify things for you.

What is one activity in your life right now you feel is weighing you down the most, keeping you from loving God with your *all?*

Something you said *yes* to, and you know it is not helping you move closer to God. It's actually moving you further from God.

One of the roles of the Holy Spirit in your life is to be your personal adviser.

When you begin doing something that is pulling you away from God, the Holy Spirit will gently and lovingly sound an alarm in you. This is what is referred to as *conviction.*

I want to encourage you to pray and ask the Holy Spirit to reveal to you any activity you've allowed into your life that may be hindering you from loving God with your *all.*

Not only does the Holy Spirit reveal to you what that hindrance may be, he also empowers you with self-control to be able to say *no* to the impulse or the desire your body may have for that thing:

> But the fruit of the Spirit is love, joy, peace, forbearance, kindness, goodness, faithfulness, gentleness and self-control. (GALATIANS 5:22–23 NIV)

You don't need more willpower to subdue the body. You need more God-power. The more of God's power you have moving in you, the more self-control you will have to tell your body *no*.

The Holy Spirit has given you overcoming strength for you to become an overcomer, but the key to living in this overcoming strength is to be filled with the Holy Spirit every day. This goes back to the practice of prayer. When you are taking the time to engage in your relationship with God each day, you immerse your whole body in the Holy Spirit. This is how you stay filled with the overcoming strength of God to subdue the body from giving in to any harmful desires

The more you say *yes* to the Spirit, the easier it is to say *no* to harmful desires.

I like to say it this way:

Subduing will prevent your undoing.

This is a great moment to introduce you to the spiritual discipline of fasting.

Fasting is the practice of intentionally abstaining from food or other pleasures for a set period of time. It is a spiritual discipline for many ancient religions, including Christianity. Scripture gives us many examples of people who chose to fast or who God called to fast, including Moses, Daniel, and, of course, Jesus.

At its core, fasting helps you discipline your cravings and strengthens what I call your resistance muscle. It allows you the opportunity to make it a habit of saying *no* to your body.

It also creates space for you to quiet the noise of everyday life and hear God's voice more clearly. For us as followers of Jesus, the practice of fasting is not just about physical discipline, but a way for us to draw closer to God, deepen our faith, and better hear his voice in our lives.

Fasting disconnects us from the distractions of the world and reconnects us with God. We don't fast to get more of God, but to give more of ourselves to God. We don't fast merely for personal breakthrough, but to break through whatever may be keeping us from God's best.

Nowhere in the Bible does it mandate fasting for followers of Jesus, but in my personal experience, there are such crazy benefits associated with fasting that I have to encourage you to pray about it. If you feel a nudge to fast, the next step would be to consult your doctor and make sure your health allows a food fast. I would also recommend you do some research on various food fasts you could practice.

If you are a person who struggles with eating disorders, I would suggest a fast that doesn't involve food. Perhaps it could be a social media fast or a spending fast. There are many options out there for fasts that don't require you to abstain from food.

At our church, we practice a twice-a-year rhythm called *twenty-one days of prayer and fasting*. We take the story of Daniel from the book of Daniel, chapter 10, in Scripture as our inspiration in doing this. (It is interesting that all kinds of research points to the fact that it takes roughly twenty-one days to form a habit in your life.) In Daniel chapter 10, Daniel doesn't abstain from all food. It reads that he was abstaining from *choice food*, which included meat, wine, and sugary foods.

Learn to work that *resistance muscle*. Have a practice of saying *no* to the cravings of your flesh.

Leaving Your Comfort Zone

WHETHER IT'S THROUGH serving, sharing, or subduing, loving God with *all* your strength is going to bring you out of your comfort zone.

Living life in the comfort zone is boring and overrated. More importantly, miracles seem to always take place outside of the comfort zone.

When you leave your comfort zone and *put it all on the line* for God, you are going to begin experiencing God in the same way the followers of Jesus did in the book of Acts.

Lives will be changed.

People will be healed.

Families will be restored.

All because you *put it all on the line* for God.

Put your seat belt on. It's going to be the greatest adventure of your life.

Strength and Conditioning

AS I CLOSE out this section on loving God with *all* your strength, I want you to know this final part of the *greatest of all time* commandment is either going to be the easiest or the most difficult for you to live out, and here is the reason why.

The first three parts of the commandment (your heart, your soul, and your mind) have to do with your internal self.

Your strength, however, is the only one in this foursome that deals with your external self. It's the only one on display for others to see.

Earlier in this book, I talked about how all four of these areas of the *GOAT* commandment are connected to each other. Think of them as a relay team. The race starts off with your soul. Your soul runs and then passes the baton to the mind. Your mind runs and passes the baton to the heart, and running anchor to finish the race is, you guessed it, your strength.

It makes sense that your strength runs anchor, because your strength is what you see in the end. Your strength is the outward expression of the love you possess in your soul, mind, and heart.

This is why if you're doing great with loving God with *all* your soul, with *all* your mind, and with *all* your heart, it's going to be easy for you to love him with *all* your strength.

On the other hand, if you are struggling with the first three, loving God with *all* your strength will be difficult, if not impossible, for you to achieve.

Let me let you in on a big pet peeve of mine.

Have you ever gone to the kitchen and opened the fridge to pour yourself a glass of your favorite beverage only to discover someone beat you to it, leaving enough in the jug to where it technically is not empty, but not enough to even fill the bottom of your glass?

Why does this happen?

Do they not want to take the time to throw something in the trash?

Do they not want to be the guilty party who drank the last of the beverage?

Why, I ask. Why?

I am convinced there is a special place in heaven for these people!

The reason I bring up this big pet peeve of mine is to first convict you if you are the guilty party who keeps doing this to the people who love you. For the love of the family, drink it all and throw out the container. Please!

More importantly, I wanted to share this with you because this is how many people are living out their faith in God.

Many people have the best intentions to live godly lives, but when they go to pour out godliness, there's just barely any substance there. All that comes out is a few measly drops that really don't make any impact at all.

The most essential piece in loving God with *all* of your strength, to live a life *putting it all on the line* for God, is to make sure your container is full to the brim. (Remember: The word *all* means completely or fully.)

When everything inside of you is full of love for God, you will have an abundance of godly things to pour out of your life.

If you are loving him with *all* your soul, *all* your mind, and *all* your heart, it's going to be easy and almost effortless to love him with *all* your strength.

Loving God with *all* your strength is so important because this is the one part of the *GOAT* commandment that makes a difference, not only for you, but also for people in and around your life. This is the part that is put on display, like a brightly lit billboard. When you are loving God with *all* your strength, you are helping point people to God.

Listen to these words of Jesus in the most famous sermon he ever preached while he was on this earth:

> You are the light of the world. A town built on a hill cannot be hidden. Neither do people light a lamp and put it under a bowl. Instead they put it on its stand, and it gives light to everyone in the house. In the same way, let your light shine before others, that they may

see your good deeds and glorify your Father in heaven.
(MATTHEW 5:14–16 NIV)

Loving God with *all* your strength becomes a beaming light for others to help lead them out of their darkness and find their way to God.

DISCUSSION QUESTIONS FOR PART 4:

All My Strength

- What does loving God with *all* your strength mean to you right now? Are there ways you feel you can show more of your ability or effort to God in your everyday life?

- Think about a time when you did something brave or went out of your comfort zone because of your new faith. What was that experience like, and how did it affect your faith journey?

- In the story of David's mighty men, they *put it all on the line* to help David. How can you apply this idea of putting all your effort into loving and serving Jesus, even if it feels risky or challenging?

- What are some small ways you can serve others or share your faith that don't require a lot of experience or preparation? How might these actions help you love God with *all* your strength?

- Jim shares a story about offering a ride to strangers as an act of love. Are there simple, everyday opportunities in your life to show love and kindness to others as an expression of your faith?

- How do you think the Holy Spirit helps or encourages you when you try to love God with your strength? Have you ever felt the Spirit guiding or helping you in a special way?

- What fears or doubts do you have about doing something radical or bold for God? How can trusting in God's presence and power help you overcome those fears?

- What talents, skills, or abilities do you have that you could use to serve others or share Jesus's love? How might you grow in using these strengths?

- Looking ahead, what is one step you can take this week to *put it all on the line* for Jesus—whether that's reaching out to someone, helping in your community, or sharing your testimony?

- What is one activity you can think of that is weighing you down and keeping you from loving God with *all* your strength? What are some practical ways you can learn to say *no* to activities that are moving you away from God?

CONCLUSION

KEEP YOUR TANK ON FULL

It's not how you start, but it's how you finish.
—MICHAEL PHELPS

B EING A RESIDENT of Southern California for most of my life, I have been consistently reminded that the big earthquake could happen at any moment. I was twenty-two years old when the 1994 Northridge earthquake happened, taking the lives of fifty-seven people and causing billions of dollars in infrastructure damage. That one literally tossed me out of my bed. So, yes, the concern is legitimate.

It has been ingrained in me to always be prepared in case disaster strikes. Have a box of emergency food on hand. Make sure to have extra jugs of water. Keep a working flashlight handy. And as much as possible, try to keep the car with a full tank of gas.

Beyond being prepared for a disaster, keeping your gas tank as full as possible, or for you electric vehicle owners, keeping it as charged as possible, is a more peaceful way to live.

It is such an awful feeling to jump in your car to drive to an appointment you are already running late to only to discover the "E" light is on. You didn't take the extra time to fill up or charge up the night before. Now you are going to be really late. It's so stressful to have to watch the "miles till empty" gauge tick down.

One time, my wife and I forgot to fill up as we left town to visit some friends. I only realized we had forgotten when the E light came on. The problem was we were over fifty miles away from the next gas station, and the miles till empty on the dashboard were at fifty.

I was praying for God to bless the gas in the tank like Jesus did with the loaves and fishes so we could make it to the next gas station. I was so mad at myself for forgetting to fill up. My wife thought my stress and frustration were the funniest thing. She just kept giggling over my freak-out session. I do believe God did a miracle on that trip, at least I choose to believe it was a miracle. The "miles till empty" on my dashboard went all the way to zero, and we were still able to make it to a gas station and fill up without running out of gas.

The point I am making here is that having a full tank, or a full charge, is the most peaceful way to live because you are always ready. You know you are going to make it to where you are supposed to go.

Our relationship with God is no different.

Living with a full tank of love for God is the most peaceful way to live.

Your ability to respond to disaster, stress, and conflict in a healthy way goes up exponentially when you're living life with the love tank on full.

This means more peaceful responses and fewer freak-out sessions.

This is what loving God with your *all* means. It's keeping yourself *full* and *whole* with the love of God.

The greatest challenge of loving God with your *all* is you tend to leak.

We all do.

The tank can be full for a while, but if we are not keeping our eyes on the gauges, we can quickly go from *full* and *whole* back down to *part* or *some*.

There is a Scripture Paul writes to the church in Ephesus that has always been a great reminder for me to make sure my life is always running full of the Spirit of God:

> Don't be drunk with wine, because that will ruin
> your life. Instead, be filled with the Holy Spirit."
> (EPHESIANS 5:18 NLT)

The word for "be filled" in the Greek is *pleroo* (pronounced play-ro'-o), and it's the present imperative form of the verb, meaning it is not a *one-and-done* thing you do. It is to be understood as a *continual action*.

Paul is telling the Ephesian church, instead of filling your tanks with alcohol, which will actually lead you to make horrible decisions with your life, *continue* to be filled with the Holy Spirit.

I love how he connects the two issues, drinking alcohol and being filled with the Spirit.

Here's my experience.

If I don't continue to be filled in my own love relationship with God and the tank goes down to half, or even worse, it drops down so low the E light comes on, I will start feeling it spiritually, mentally, emotionally, and even sometimes physically. My propensity in those moments is to grab whatever is the easiest thing in front of me to fill the emptiness. I think, for the Ephesian church, it must have been excessive drinking of wine.

The fuller you are living in the love of God, the less desire you will have to get drunk, or fill your life with other unhelpful things.

This means loving God with your *all* is not only unlocking the promises of God for your life, loving God with your *all* is also un-hitching you from damaging habits in your life.

Looking at the gauges on your life dashboard, where is the needle with your love for God?

Is it on full?

Is it in the middle?

Or, perhaps is the "E" light on?

I want to finish up with one final sobering word Jesus gave to one of the seven churches mentioned in the final book in our Bibles, the book of Revelation.

The church in Ephesus was doing some mighty good things for God. They get a lot of compliments from Jesus, but the passage goes from high praise to a hard rebuke:

> But I have this against you, that you have abandoned the love you had at first. Remember therefore from where you have fallen; repent, and do the works you did at first. (REVELATION 2:4–5 ESV)

This same church that Paul encourages to stay filled up, Jesus is now saying, "Somewhere on the journey, you guys started running with the E light on."

They had it for a while. They were loving God with their *all*, but somehow, someway, they began to get emptied.

This word isn't just for the church in Ephesus; this is for all of us who follow Jesus.

I know many people who have started out with their tanks on full. They were loving God with their *all*, but somehow, someway, their tanks began to empty over time.

It seems like these past ten years or so, the American church has experienced the moral failures of quite a few spiritual giants of our time. Men of God who have done incredible things for God's kingdom, made ungodly decisions that inevitably led them to lose their platforms of leadership in the church, and in some cases, their marriages along with it.

These men now stand as cautionary tales for all of us.

In the words of the *greatest of all time* Olympic gold medalist, Michael Phelps, "It's not how you start that's important. It's how you finish that matters."

One of my favorite proverbs in Scripture says it this way:

> Finishing is better than starting. (ECCLESIASTES 7:8 NLT)

I look at every one of these fallen leaders of faith as a reminder that the way I loved God last year is irrelevant to my love for him right now.

Loving God with your *all* is something you must check on continually.

This is how you check the gauge of your love tank. Ask yourself this question:

"Has there ever been a time in the history of me being a follower of Jesus that I have loved Jesus more than I love him right now?"

If the answer is yes, chances are you have fallen into this same position as the church of Ephesus did, and for whatever reason, your tank has emptied out from the love that you had at the beginning.

As you consider what it looks like to love God with your all, I want you to see there's a call of God in this passage to come back to that love you had at the beginning.

Remember when you first were introduced to Jesus?

When somebody first talked to you about the grace of God and how he wanted to heal you?

How he wanted to set you free?

When you embraced that healing?

When you encountered for the first time the incredible love that God has for you?

It was new.

It was exciting.

It was the best thing that ever happened to you.

You couldn't wait to get up in the morning and have a quiet time with God.

You couldn't wait to get to church to hear what the Holy Spirit was going to speak to your heart.

You couldn't wait to open your Bible and hear what the Spirit of God was going to speak to you through the pages of Scripture.

You were pumped to tell your family and friends about Jesus.

You were inviting everyone you knew to come to a church gathering with you.

You were crazy in love with God. God is calling you back to love him like that again.

It's not how you start that matters. It's how you finish.

How do you get it back? How do you fill the tank again?

According to how Jesus coached the church of Ephesus, start by going back and doing the things you did before.

That's how simple it is to be filled up and back in the status of loving God with your *all*.

Don't settle for loving God a little bit, or with some, or even part.

Make a decision to go back to the start and renew your love for God with your *all*.

Some married couples who have been through difficulties and hardships find it helpful to renew their vows to help reignite their relationship and give it a fresh start.

Tara and I did this ourselves for our twenty-fifth wedding anniversary. We took the kids with us and we renewed our vows on the beach in Maui, Hawaii. A Hawaiian pastor led us through some vows as the sun was setting behind us. It was an epic ceremony that even included a ukulele.

Renewing yourself in any relationship is important, and it's a choice you can make every day, not just on special anniversaries. While our trip to Maui was amazing, Tara and I make it a point to renew our love regularly—through date nights and long conversations at night. These moments help keep our love strong.

As you consider the most important relationship in your life, your relationship with your creator, I encourage you to renew your commitment with him, to love him with *all* your soul, with *all* your mind, with *all* your heart, and with *all* your strength.

Do the things you did at the beginning.

Love him with your *soul* by renewing yourself to spend time talking with him and connecting with him.

Love him with your *mind* by renewing yourself to opening the

Scriptures daily and journaling all God wants to reveal to you.

Love him with your *heart* by renewing yourself in worship to him. To sing to him, to give to him, and to live for him.

Love him with your *strength* by renewing yourself to be activated for him. Step out and *put it all on the line* for him.

As you renew yourself to loving God with your *all* in all four of these cylinders (spiritually, mentally, emotionally, and physically), you will discover it is the way to keep the tank full.

Living this way prevents the love tank from ever running out. As a matter of fact, living this way increases the capacity of your tank so your love for God actually increases.

As you begin experiencing his promises, hearing from heaven, walking in miracles, having your own God stories, your love for God is going to grow stronger.

My life has been forever changed by living out this *GOAT* commandment. I don't live it out perfectly. No one does. However, I have seen firsthand the blessings of living in the promises of God. So much so that even when I stumble, I feel the grace of God pick me back up and I go straight back to where I need to be, loving him with my *all*.

Even if you have been away from God for a while. Maybe you are thinking, *There is no way God would pick me back up.* I want to declare to you something you need to hear as I wrap up this book. God's grace is greater than your greatest mistake. He loves you! Let his love for you soak in.

After you let that love saturate your soul, love him back with your whole being, and his promises will start moving in every area of your life.

The key to unlocking the door to these promises of God for your life is not found in loving him with your part, or even with your some.

It's only found when you are loving him with your *all*.

DISCUSSION QUESTIONS FOR THE CONCLUSION
Keep Your Tank on Full

- What does it mean to keep your *tank* full in your relationship with God? How do you think loving God with your *all* can bring peace into your daily life?

- Just like we need to keep our cars' gas tanks full, why is it important to regularly *refill* our spiritual love for God? What are some practical ways you can do this daily or weekly?

- The chapter mentions that loving God with your *all* is a continual process ("be filled with the Holy Spirit"). What are some habits or practices that can help you stay connected to God and keep your tank full?

- Have you ever felt like your faith or relationship with God was "running on empty"? What steps can you take to *refill* your love for God when you feel this way?

- The church in Ephesus started out loving God passionately, but later *fell away* from that love. What are some signs in your life that could indicate your love for God is starting to fade? How can you recognize and address these signs early?

- The chapter encourages going back to "what you did at the beginning" to rekindle your love for God. What were some of the things you did when you first became a follower of Jesus that helped you feel close to God? Are you willing to do those again?

- Renewal and recommitment are important in any relationship, including with God. How can you intentionally renew your love for God today? Are there specific actions or decisions you can make?

- The chapter talks about the importance of checking the *gauges* of your love for God. How can you regularly evaluate where you are spiritually? What questions can you ask yourself to do this honestly?

- Why do you think it's easy to start strong in loving God but harder to finish well? What can help you stay committed to loving God with your *all* over the long run?

ACKNOWLEDGMENTS

First and foremost, I want to thank my incredible wife, Tara Crews. We have been married for thirty-three years, and she has been my best friend, my partner in life, and my greatest supporter. Throughout the seasons of my life, she has been my biggest encourager, and, most recently, the chief editor of this book. I am deeply grateful for her steadfast presence by my side.

To my children—Kylee, McKenzee, and Josiah—thank you for being such wonderful kids and even better adults. Your patience and willingness to be used as examples in so many sermons throughout the years have meant the world to me. Watching you grow into such amazing adults and seeing you love Jesus with your all has been one of my greatest joys.

A special thank you to my father-in-law, Ron Vietti, who has been my spiritual mentor and pastor since I was eighteen. His example of loving God with all his heart has profoundly shaped my understanding of what it truly means to follow Christ with every part of my being.

I also want to express my gratitude to my team of beta readers— Dr. Geoff Buckley, Milad Girgis, and Heidi Rogers—whose insights and encouragement helped refine this book into what it is today.

Finally, I am thankful for the three amazing church families I have been privileged to be a part of Valley Bible in Bakersfield, California; Valley Vegas in Las Vegas, Nevada; and Atmosphere

Church in Thousand Oaks, California. Through these beautiful communities, I have had the privilege of leading and discipling hundreds of people in their journey of learning to love God with their *all*. This book is the fruit of decades of discipleship, prayer, and God's faithfulness.

To everyone who has walked alongside me on this journey—thank you. This book is dedicated to you and to the pursuit of unlocking God's promises for your life.

ABOUT THE AUTHOR

Jim Crews is a dynamic and influential leader in the Christian community, with over thirty years of full-time ministry that has impacted thousands of lives. As a visionary pastor and church planter, Jim has helped launch two thriving, life-giving churches—one in Las Vegas, where he served as lead pastor for over a decade, and most recently, Atmosphere Church in Thousand Oaks, California. His profound insights into spiritual growth and leadership have been featured in top ministry publications. He has also been a featured speaker at conferences, crusades, and Christian camps across the globe. Married to Tara for thirty-three years, Jim is a proud father of three adult children, two of whom are now married, and recently celebrated the joys of grandparenthood. Besides his love for God and his family, Jim also has a love for college football and anything related to the 1980s.

ENDNOTES

1   The Shema prayer is one of the most famous prayers in the Bible. It was a daily prayer for ancient Israelites and is still recited by Jewish people today. The Shema gets its name from the first Hebrew word of the prayer—"hear" or "listen," a translation of the Hebrew word shema. Ancient Jewish people combined lines from Deuteronomy 6:4–5 with other passages from the Torah (Deuteronomy 11:13–21; Numbers 15:37–41) and prayed these words every morning and every evening. This prayer has been one of the most influential traditions in Jewish history, functioning both as the Jewish pledge of allegiance and a hymn of praise. For further study on the Shema, I recommend checking out the link below from the Bible project: https://bibleproject.com/articles/what-is-the-shema/.

2   Dwight L. Moody (1837–1899) was a prominent American evangelist and publisher who played a significant role in the revival movements of the late nineteenth century. Born in Massachusetts to a poor family, he initially worked as a shoe salesman before experiencing a spiritual awakening that led him to dedicate his life to preaching. Moody founded the Moody Bible Institute in Chicago, which aimed to train laypeople for evangelism. He was known for his powerful sermons and ability to connect with diverse audiences, emphasizing personal faith and the need for social reform.

3   Duncan MacDougall, "The Soul: Hypothesis Concerning Soul Substance Together with Experimental Evidence of the Existence of Such Substance," *American Medicine* 2: 240–243.

4   Quote by Deion Sanders, https://www.toledoblade.com/news/religion/2002/11/30/Deion-Sanders-finds-peace-in-God-s-game-plan/stories/200211300009.

5   Death Cab for Cutie (commonly abbreviated to DCFC or Death Cab) is an American indie rock band formed in Bellingham, Washington, in 1997. I do not know whether the band or band members identify as being Christians, but their song definitely spoke to me as if the Lord were speaking to me. God uses all kinds of ways and things to speak to us, including indie rock bands.

6   Because I wasn't able to obtain permission from the publisher to use the actual lyrics of the song in this book, I had to summarize the part that hit me the hardest, but at some point today, please google the lyrics yourself and you will see exactly why these lyrics hit me so deep.

7 Brother Lawrence, *The Practice of the Presence of God* (Whitaker House, 1982).

8 Matthew 26:26–28, Mark 14:22–24, Luke 22:19–20, and 1 Corinthians 11:23–26.

9 To find out more about the term *trinity* and its origin story within Christianity, visit https://www.gotquestions.org/origin-doctrine-Trinity.html.

10 Billy Graham, *The Holy Spirit* (W Pub Group, 1978).

11 Charles Spurgeon was a nineteenth-century preacher from London known by many as the "prince of preachers." Many of his famous quotes, including this one, can be found at a website dedicated to his legacy: https://www.princeofpreachers.org/quotes/archives/05-2017/2.

12 Mark Batterson, *The Circle Maker* (Zondervan, 2016).

13 There have been multiple studies done trying to discover just how many thoughts we experience each day. This is why there is a spectrum of numbers experts give when reporting how many thoughts the average human has per day. Here are a few links to some of the latest studies done on the subject: https://www.healthline.com/health/how-many-thoughts-per-day#thoughts-per-day; https://www.newsweek.com/humans-6000-thoughts-every-day-1517963; https://healthybrains.org/wp-content/uploads/2015/05/08000536/BrainHealthGuide.pdf.

14 Neuroplasticity is the ability of the nervous system to change its activity in response to intrinsic or extrinsic stimuli by reorganizing its structure, functions, or connections." https://pmc.ncbi.nlm.nih.gov/articles/PMC6400842/.

15 https://www.centerforbibleengagement.org/_files/ugd/c59c7d_efca2bdec49a4bc69e6056a2355760b9.pdf.

16 https://1s712.americanbible.org/state-of-the-bible/stateofthebible/State_of_the_bible-2022.pdf.

17 https://memorylab.nd.edu/assets/258700/bohay_blakely_tamplin_radvansky_2011_american_journal_of_psychology_.pdf.

18 Charles Spurgeon was a nineteenth century preacher from London known by many as the "prince of preachers." Many of his famous quotes, including this one, can be found at a website dedicated to his legacy. https://www.princeofpreachers.org/quotes/archives/05-2017/2.

19 http://www.apa.org/news/press/releases/2015/04/grateful-heart.aspx.

20 http://www.ncbi.nlm.nih.gov/pubmed/19073292.

21 The Blue Letter Bible App is a great resource for your study of the Bible. One of my favorite features about this app is it allows you easy access to the definitions and pronunciations of the Hebrew and Greek words in the Bible.

22 Heart disease has been the leading cause of death in the United States since 1950. https://www.cdc.gov/nchs/hus/topics/heart-disease-deaths.htm.

23 Alexithymia is when a person has difficulty experiencing, identifying, and expressing emotions. https://www.healthline.com/health/autism/alexithymia.

24 The *GOAT* love song—"Endless Love," Diana Ross and Lionel Richie, https://www.billboard.com/lists/top-love-songs-all-time/ill-make-love-to-you-boyz-ii-men-hot-100-peak-no-1-for-14-weeks-1994-2/.

25 Los Angeles is the sixth most expensive city in the world to live in: https://www.forbes.com/sites/laurabegleybloom/2023/11/30/ranked-the-worlds-10-most-expensive-cities-to-live-according-to-a-new-report/.

26 The science behind the "helper's high," https://greatergood.berkeley.edu/article/item/how_volunteering_can_help_your_mental_health.

27 Modern-day Satanism and the practice of "Do whatever thou wilt." https://digitalcommons.usu.edu/cgi/viewcontent.cgi?article=1076&context=imwjournal.

www.ingramcontent.com/pod-product-compliance
Lightning Source LLC
Chambersburg PA
CBHW031459120626
46545CB00005B/1674